Whirlpool

Micro Menus Cookbook

This cookbook will help you learn the principles of microwave cooking. In the first section we'll explain what microwaves are, how they work and how to use them to best advantage. In the second major section (Breakfast, Lunch and Dinner), we start you cooking with step-by-step instructions and illustrations. The third section, an alphabetized selection of great-tasting recipes, is more advanced and includes a number of helpful charts for convenient future reference.

Pictured on the cover: Teriyaki Chicken on a bed of parsley rice. (See chicken roasting directions on page 102. Brush chicken with bottled teriyaki sauce twice during roasting.)

NOTE: Be sure that you carefully read and that you understand the Use and Care booklet that came with your microwave oven before starting to use the oven. It contains operating instructions, safety recommendations, and other important information about the proper use of your microwave oven.

PRECAUTIONS TO AVOID POSSIBLE EXPOSURE TO EXCESSIVE MICROWAVE ENERGY

- Do not attempt to operate this oven with the door open since open-door operation can result in harmful exposure to microwave energy. It is important not to defeat or tamper with the safety interlocks.
- Do not place any object between the oven front face and the door or allow soil or cleaner residue to accumulate on sealing surfaces.
- Do not operate the oven if it is damaged. It is particularly important that the oven door close properly and that there is no damage to the: (1) door (bent), (2) hinges and latches (broken or loosened), (3) door seals and sealing surfaces.
- The oven should not be adjusted or repaired by anyone except properly qualified service personnel.
- The oven should be checked for microwave leakage by qualified service personnel after a repair is made.
- Do not operate the oven if the door glass is broken.
- Do not operate the microwave oven with the outer cabinet removed.

IF YOU NEED SERVICE OR ASSISTANCE, WE SUGGEST YOU FOLLOW THESE 4 STEPS.

1. Before calling for assistance...
Check the things you can do yourself. Refer to the literature furnished with your appliance to insure it is correctly installed and you are familiar with its normal operation.

2. If you need assistance...*
Call the Whirlpool COOL-LINE service assistance telephone number. Dial free from:

Continental U.S. .... (800) 253-130

Michigan .... (800) 632-224

Alaska & Hawaii .... (800) 253-112

and talk with one of our trained Consultants. The Consultant can instruct you on how to obtain satisfactory operation from your appliance or, if service is necessary, recommend a qualified service company in your area.

3. If you need service...*

Whirlpool has a nationwide network of franchised TECH-CARE Service Companies. TECH-CARE service technicians are trained to fulfill the product warranty and provide after-warranty service, anywhere in the United States.

To locate TECH-CARE service in your area, call our COOL-LINE service assistance telephone number (See Step 2) **or look in your telephone directory Yellow Pages under:**

| APPLIANCES-HOUSEHOLD-MAJOR-SERVICE & REPAIR | OR | ELECTRICAL APPLIANCES-MAJOR-REPAIRING & PARTS | OR | WASHING MACHINES, DRYER & IRONERS-SERVICING |

4. If you have a problem...*
Call our COOL-LINE service assistance telephone number (see Step 2) and talk with one of our Consultants, or if you prefer, write to

Mr. Guy Turner, Vice President
Whirlpool Corporation
Administrative Center
2000 US-33 North
Benton Harbor, MI 49022

*If you must call or write, please provide: model number, serial number, date of purchase, and a complete description of the problem. This information is needed in order to better respond to your request for assistance.

Contents

Copyright© 1981, Litton Systems, Inc.
Printed in the United States of America.

6 7 8 9 10 11 12 D 9 8 7 6

The Whats and Hows of Microwaves

Here's what microwaves are, how they work and how they compare with other methods of cooking.

What are microwaves?

Microwaves are electromagnetic waves that are classified as being of a "non-ionizing" frequency which means they do not cause a chemical change (as do "ionizing" rays such as x-rays). Electrical and natural waves are all around us—radio and TV signals, and even sunlight arrives in waves. Any form of energy transmitted by waves must have a frequency. These frequencies are all stated in a scientific form called the Electromagnetic Spectrum. Here, frequencies are expressed as cycles per second. The number of cycles per second is the number of times the wave dips above and below an imaginary base line, (positve and negative). The higher the frequency, the shorter the wave. The shorter the wave, the more cycles it can produce in a second. For cooking, the cycle occurs at 2½ billion times a second. Microwaves used for cooking pass through glass, paper, plastic and wood. But they can't penetrate metal, and instead bounce off at angles.

Molecular action in food.

All food and liquid molecules have positive and negative particles which are in constant—but slow—motion. (Positive and negatives attract and repel each other like magnets.) In microwave cooking this molecular action is then accelerated. The instant microwaves bombard food they agitate the molecules. Agitation causes friction as molecules rub and bump into each other at a frenzied rate. And friction results in heat that cooks food and boils water. A similar action happens when you rub your hands together.

Once the microwaves stop, this friction action continues by itself—eventually tapering off and returning to normal molecular action. Later on you'll learn how this principle works to your advantage in standing and holding times.

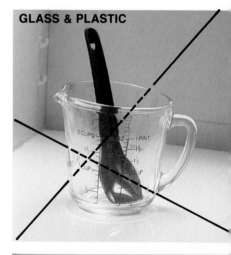

GLASS & PLASTIC

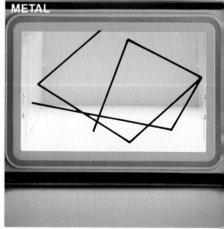

METAL

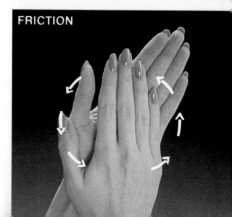

FRICTION

MICROWAVE OVEN

SURFACE UNIT

CONVENTIONAL OVEN

How do they work?

There are many misconceptions about how microwaves "cook" food. Actually, microwaves penetrate food to a depth of ¾ to 1½ inches. As cooking begins, heat is spread by conduction to the interior portion of the food . . . just as in conventional cooking methods. Your microwave oven features variable power settings that allow you to choose the speed at which food cooks. They are graduated settings much like the low-medium-high settings on your conventional range. The power settings are **WARM, DEFROST (Med. Low), MEDIUM (Simmer), MED. HIGH (Roast), REHEAT** and **HIGH,** with **WARM** being the lowest and **HIGH** the highest.

How do they work in my oven?

A magnetron tube in the oven converts electrical energy to microwave energy and directs that energy at a "stirrer" (similar to a fan) which evenly diffuses microwaves into the oven interior. This eliminates the need for a turntable. Since your oven is metal (covered by a glass ceramic shelf on the bottom) microwaves also bounce off the walls and the bottom into the food. They bounce off the door, too, thanks to a metal screen in the glass. Also, microwaves do not accumulate—in the food or in the oven. They're simply a source of heat energy.

How does microwave cooking compare with conventional cooking?

Conventional ovens and range tops also cause cooking in food by molecular action. But microwaves do it faster than conventional methods because microwaves move directly through the air and utensils to the food where they force the food to generate its own heat. On the range top, a saucepan placed over a flame or heating element uses conduction. (The pan must be heated before cooking can begin.) In a conventional oven, the surrounding air must be heated first to heat the dish and cook the food. This is convection. Each method cooks from the outside in, but in microwave cooking (radiant heat) the energy only affects the food and does not heat the surrounding air or dish. However, heat from the food in prolonged cooking will heat the utensil.

But Before You Begin...

...Safety comes first. Your conventional oven has its own list of do-nots, and so does your microwave. Some relate directly to the unique features of the oven, but most are simply common sense precautions.·

For example, many recipes will have you cover foods with wax paper or plastic wrap. To avoid steam burns, be careful when removing the covers. Also, while microwave ovens don't generate heat to cook food, both the food and possibly the container will become hot. So use hot pads. That's common sense! Here are more:

DO NOT use the oven for storage. Paper products, newspapers, books or cooking utensils don't belong in the oven when not in use.

DO NOT use the oven as a timer. (Unless your oven has the Minute Timer feature.)

DO NOT let the timer continue to operate after removing food.

DO NOT run the oven without food in it. Such accidental use for short periods of time won't damage the oven, but it isn't recommended.

DO NOT attempt to cook or reheat eggs in or out of the shell; they may explode. In rare instances, poached eggs have also been known to explode. Please follow instructions for covering and the standing time of one minute before cutting into poached eggs.

DO NOT try to can foods in your microwave oven. Closed jars may explode.

DO NOT overcook foods. Overcooking certain foods like potatoes (see page 118 for cooking times) may result in fire which can damage the oven interior. Start with the minimum cooking times given in the recipe

and if you must add additional time to properly cook the item, watch it closely. In case of fire, unplug the oven and keep the door closed.

DO NOT use metal pots, pans or baking sheets; dishes trimmed with gold or silver; foil trays deeper than ¾ of an inch; or any glass or ceramic utensil with metal screws, bands or handles.

DO NOT use metal twist-ties in your microwave oven. When cooking or defrosting in plastic bags, remove any metal twist-ties to prevent arcing. (See utensil chart, pages 10 and 11.)

DO NOT use melamine dishes. They become hot in the microwave—often too hot to handle. And food takes longer to cook, too.

DO NOT leave oven unattended during short cooking times. Overcooking and possible fire may result.

DO NOT reheat food in foil-lined containers (the take-out/doggie bag kind).

DO NOT pop popcorn unless popped in a microwave approved popcorn popper or unless it's commercially packaged and recommended especially for microwave ovens. There are too many variables—things such as time, temperature and age of popcorn. Regardless of popcorn age, microwaves pop too few kernels to make the technique successful. Prolonged cooking does not yield more popped corn, but can cause fire or make the cooking dish too hot to handle, and can even break. Never attempt to pop corn in a paper bag. Oil plus extended cooking can cause smoking and, eventually, fire.

DO NOT attempt to use the oven for purposes other than food preparation. For example: **Do not** sterilize baby bottles, **do not** melt paraffin wax in the oven and **do not** attempt to dry flowers, fruit, herbs, wood or gourds in the oven.

WARNING: Liquids may overheat without boiling, resulting in injury to you or your oven. Always boil and stir liquids when heating and reheating.

READ AND FOLLOW OTHER IMPORTANT SAFETY INSTRUCTIOINS IN YOUR USE AND CARE MANUAL.

Begin With What You Have...

Good news! Many of the utensils you'll use in your new oven are already in your kitchen. And some are items you've never dreamed of putting in an oven before. As you progress, of course, you'll want to add items like a microwave roasting rack, browning grill, muffin pans and other utensils made especially for microwave ovens. But first, begin with what you have:

GLASS: Oven-proof glass or glass ceramic baking dishes are the most-used microwave cooking utensils.

Use glass, sturdy china and pottery serving dishes only if there's no silver, gold, platinum or other metal trim or signature on the bottom.

In general, when in doubt about any glass, pottery or china utensil, do the dish test (see page 10).

PLASTICS: Dishwasher-safe plastics, hard plastic trays, picnic ware, thermal cups, mugs and bowls may be used in the oven for short periods of time. Plastic foam cups and dishes may also be used. And plastic baby bottles are safe for heating milk or formula. But none of these should be used in the oven for prolonged periods because distortion and melting may occur. Check manufacturer's recommendations.

Use plastic wrap as a tight covering, but pierce it **before removing** to prevent steam burns. Plastic cooking pouches should be slit **before cooking** so excess steam can escape.

PAPER: Paper cups, plates, towels and paper cartons should be used only for heating or defrosting. Prolonged time in the oven can cause paper to burn. Wax paper can be used as a covering during cooking.

And Then Add More

STRAW: Baskets can be used in the oven for the very short time it takes to heat rolls.

METAL: In general, metal utensils should not be used in your oven. Microwaves cannot pass through metal and food will cook only from the top, or not at all if completely enclosed in foil. But there are exceptions under certain conditions. Be sure, though, that metal does not touch oven surfaces because this could cause arcing and result in fire or pitting of the oven interior.

TV dinner trays, less than ¾ of an inch deep, are allowable because they are shallow enough for microwaves to penetrate and cook food from the top. Metal skewers and clamps are also usable when the proportion of food is much greater than metal (a well filled kebob or clamps and clips on turkeys).

Small pieces of aluminum foil can be used for shielding portions of whole poultry or roasts which are cooking too quickly. If arcing occurs, remove foil.

WOOD: Moisture in wooden utensils evaporates during microwave cooking and will cause wood to crack. However, wooden spoons or wood-handled rubber spatulas can be left in the oven for short periods of time.

MEAT/CANDY THERMOMETERS: Use only microwave meat and candy thermometers during actual cooking. Conventional thermometers may be inserted after food is removed from the oven. (Mercury in conventional thermometers reflect microwaves and make them inaccurate.)

For more specifics, turn to the chart on the next two pages.

Utensil Chart

Check this chart for the dishes which can or cannot be used in a microwave oven. If in doubt about any glass, pottery or china utensil without metal trim, do the **Dish Test:** Place dish in oven on **HIGH** for **15 to 20 seconds.** If the container feels warm when taken from the oven, do not cook or heat in it.

UTENSIL	RECOMMENDED USES
GLASS AND CHINA	
Baby bottles	Warm formula; remove lid and nipple.
Bone or other fine china	Not recommended.
Browning grill	Sear, grill and fry small meat items. Special coating on bottom of dishes allows them to absorb microwaves and preheat to high temperatures.
Centura dinnerware	Not recommended. Dishes absorb microwaves, become too hot to handle and may eventually crack or break.
Clay pot, with lid	Presoak in water, as for conventional cooking. Use for braising meats and poultry.
Correlle Livingware dinnerware	Heat cooked food, beverages, soup. Closed-handle cups should not be used; microwaves may melt adhesives.
Corning glass ceramic cooking dishes, with glass covers	Cook vegetables, meats, main dishes, desserts. Utensils may also be used for conventional cooking.
Earthenware (ironstone) dinnerware without metal trim*	Heat cooked food and beverages. Dish thickness does not affect microwave penetration. If dish is refrigerated, food takes longer to heat because heavy cold dish absorbs heat from food.
Glass or china dinnerware without metal trim*	Heat cooked food and beverages, usually without affecting dishes. Some paints or glazes used on glass dishes do contain metallic substances and should not be used in a microwave oven. See test in chart introduction.
Lead crystal	Not recommended; metal in this fine glass may cause breakage.
Pottery dishes without metal trim*	Heat cooked food, beverages and soups. Unglazed pottery may absorb moisture and heat up. See test in chart introduction.
Oven-proof Pyrex and all other oven-proof glass dishes and fitted covers, mixing bowls and measures—without metal trim*	Cook vegetables, meats, sauces, desserts, main dishes.
METAL	
Foil pie plate	Not recommended if pans are more than ¾ inch deep. Transfer food to glass pie plate.
Foil sheet	Not recommended in quantity. Foil reflects microwaves and may cause arcing that pits oven interior. Small pieces may be used to cover portions of whole poultry or roasts which appear to be cooking too quickly.
Metal spoons (not silver or gold-colored alloy)	May be left in 1 cup (or more) of sauce or pudding for short cooking periods without causing arcing.
Microwave food thermometer	Use in the microwave oven during cooking to measure temperature of food.
Pewter or silver dishes	Not recommended; they will tarnish.
Pots and pans	Not recommended. No time saved—metal reflects microwaves so food can only cook from top surface.
Skewers and poultry clamps	Safe in the oven when used with large quantities of food. Do not allow to touch sides of oven or arcing may result.
TV dinner foil trays, up to ¾ inch deep	Heat commercial or homemade frozen dinners. Food depth is shallow enough to heat through from the top.
Twist-ties for cooking bags	Not recommended, will cause arcing and melt plastic bag or create fire if associated with paper.

UTENSIL	RECOMMENDED USES
STRAW AND WOOD	
Baskets, straw or wooden	Use only for short-time heating of breads and rolls.
Cutting boards and bowls, wooden	Not recommended. Microwaves cause natural moisture in wood to evaporate, causing drying and cracking.
Spoons, wooden	Leave in puddings and sauces when stirring is needed during short cooking. Material can withstand microwaves for a short time.
PAPER	
Fast food cartons with metal handles	Not recommended; handles may cause arcing.
Foil-lined or foil-wrapped containers	Some frozen juice cans are wrapped with foil coated paper; some paper cartons, such as those for egg substitutes, are foil lined. Not recommended; foil reflects microwaves and inhibits heating.
Frozen juice containers	Defrost juice in plain paper containers. Remove one metal end, the other may be left in place during thawing in the oven.
Napkins	Heat sandwiches, rolls, doughnuts, absorb excess moisture.
Plates and cups	Heat cooked food and beverages for short periods of time; absorb moisture.
Wax paper	Use to cover cooking dishes. Will not adhere to hot food, although hot food may cause wax to partially melt and adhere to dish. Wax is not harmful if eaten.
Towel	Use when heating breads to absorb moisture. Not recommended when cooking 4 or more slices of bacon as some towels are made of recycled materials and may contain metal particles which can cause fire when soaked with fat.
PLASTIC	
Baby bottles	Warm formula; remove lid and nipple.
Boilable bags	Use when freezing food, then reheating in bag. Slit bag; remove twist-tie.
Cooking pouches	Cook vegetables, rice, meats and other frozen foods. Slit pouch so steam escapes; however, seal on bag is made to withstand low pressure so will not explode if bag is accidently not slit.
Foam cups and dishes	Heat beverages and precooked foods for short periods. Long heating makes food hot and it melts plastic foam.
Melamine dishes	Not recommended. Dishes become hot, often too hot to handle. Food takes longer to cook.
Microwave roasting rack	Roast meat, poultry; heat sandwiches. Holds food above cooking dish moisture and drippings.
Oven film and cooking bags	Film without foil edges is suitable for roasts and stews. Bag, itself, will not cause tenderizing. Use a rubber band or string in place of metal twist-tie to prevent arcing.
Plastic wrap	Use to cover cooking dishes when a tight covering is needed and a dish has no fitted glass cover. Always puncture wrap and allow steam to escape before removing wrap from a dish of hot food.
Popcorn poppers	Use only microwave approved products. Follow manufacturers' instructions carefully.
Soft plastic, such as dessert topping containers	Use only dishwasher-proof containers for storage, then reheating, cooked food. These containers withstand most lower temperatures reached in heating.
Spatulas and spoons	May be left in 1 cup (or more) of food during short-time cooking. Wood handles may become hot.
Tupperware	Not recommended; it distorts easily.

*Dishes with gold, silver, platinum or other metal trim including signatures on dish bottoms should not be used during microwave cooking or they may break.

Food Characteristics:
How Microwaves Affect Them

The food characteristics illustrated on these pages affect all types of cooking. But the increased speed of microwave cooking makes differences even more pronounced.

Before you start microwaving, ask yourself two basic questions: What do I want to do with the food I'm putting in the oven? Do I want it defrosted, heated or cooked? And, what are the characteristics of that food?

One important characteristic is quantity. It takes longer to heat a pitcher of apple cider than it takes to heat a cup of cider. Another characteristic is starting temperature. It takes longer to heat refrigerated cider than it does to heat an equal quantity of room temperature cider.

Awareness of food characteristics is important for best results, which is why we've given them to you. On the other hand, don't feel like you need an advanced degree in chemistry before operating your microwave! In explaining why certain things happen the way they do, we feel you'll be happier with the results of your cooking, and there will be fewer surprises.

WATER attracts microwaves and during cooking is drawn to the surface of food. This moisture will evaporate on the surface. Cakes and breads microwave with tender surfaces and do not brown.

FAT attracts microwaves. Large roasts, turkeys and chickens brown during prolonged cooking as their natural fats are drawn to the surface. The centers of these foods are cooked by heat conduction. While smaller portions of meat—hamburger patties, steaks, chops—also contain fat, their cooking time is not long enough for browning to take place.

SUGAR also attracts microwaves. As the thermometers show, the high-sugar jelly center of the sweet roll rises to a much higher temperature than the cake portion containing less sugar. Care should be taken in heating so that the center doesn't burn...and in the eating because the center is hotter than the rest of the roll.

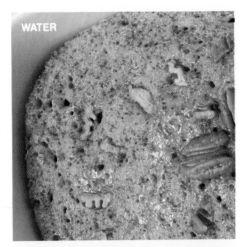
WATER

FAT

SUGAR

120°F   100°F

QUANTITY

DENSITY

STARTING TEMPERATURE

QUANTITY determines cooking time. Small amounts of food or liquid require less cooking time than larger amounts of the same substance. That's because small quantities receive concentrated amounts of microwaves. As quantity increases, concentration decreases. If you double a recipe, increase the time by about half and check for doneness.

DENSITY differences are illustrated here by a slice of bread and a slice of meat. The bread is light and airy while the meat is heavy and compact with a great deal more substance. As you would suspect, dense, heavy foods take longer to microwave than lighter foods because microwaves cannot penetrate as deeply and the food must heat by conduction from the hot outer edges. The slice of meat heats in 2 to 3 minutes while the bread takes just 20 to 30 seconds.

STARTING TEMPERATURE is another common sense principle. Room temperature foods cook faster than refrigerated foods. And refrigerated foods cook faster than frozen foods. A package of frozen stew will obviously take longer to cook than a can of stew at room temperature. Remember too, that room temperatures vary with the time of year and that cooking times may be longer on cold winter days.

Differences in **LINE VOLTAGE** to your home may cause differences in heating or cooking times in your oven. For instance, a cup of coffee may take 1½ minutes to heat one day and 2 minutes the next day. This is normal, as the line voltage varies from household to household, day to day, time of day and season to season. 13

Food Characteristics:

SIZE of food to be microwaved follows the same line of reasoning as quantity. Small pieces cook faster than larger pieces of food. The steak, shown cut into strips, will cook from all sides...faster than the whole steak which is larger and cooks through to the center by conduction (Remember that microwaves penetrate food ¾ to 1½ inches.)

SHAPE is another determining factor in speed of cooking. Many foods are uneven—like a chicken, ribs or broccoli. The thin parts will cook faster than the thick parts while uniformly thick foods cook evenly. To compensate, place slower-to-cook, dense portions near the outside of the dish where cooking takes place first. Thin, less dense parts placed toward the center of the dish receive less microwave energy. Or, shield thin parts with small pieces of aluminum foil to slow cooking.

QUALITY is one characteristic that proves your oven is not completely magic. The same principles apply here as in conventional cooking. It won't make canned vegetables taste like fresh, or round steak as tender as T-bone steak. The quality of food you put in will determine what you get out. Good quality, fresh meat and vegetables microwave best in terms of taste, texture and appearance.

SIZE

SHAPE

QUALITY

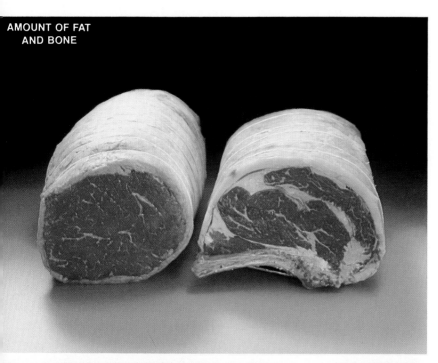

AMOUNT OF FAT AND BONE

SENSITIVE INGREDIENTS

AMOUNT OF FAT AND BONE
determine how rapidly and evenly meat cuts will cook. Because bones conduct heat, the side of meat the bone is on will cook first, while boneless cuts cook slower but more evenly. Use the two roasts pictured as examples. Since fat attracts microwave energy, evenly distributed fat will tenderize and help meat cook evenly as in the first roast pictured. But a large, fatty area as shown by the second roast will attract microwaves away from the meat and slow cooking times.

SENSITIVE INGREDIENTS
include cheese, eggs, cream, sour cream, condensed milk, mayonnaise, snails, oysters, chicken livers, kidney beans and mushrooms. These overcook very quickly and can toughen, curdle or "pop". Watch for this term throughout this book. Use lower power settings, **MED. HIGH (Roast)** or lower when sensitive foods are microwaved alone or added to a mixture.

Microwave Techniques

Most techniques you'll use in microwave cooking are carryovers from conventional cooking. Here they are for review...as well as some new ones to consider.

Pictured: Chili, recipe page 87.

STIRRING

TURNING

ARRANGEMENT

ARRANGEMENT

REARRANGEMENT

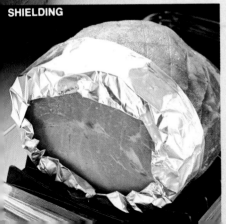

SHIELDING

STIRRING is kept at a minimum in variable power ovens with their lower energy settings. An even cooking pattern in your microwave oven also minimizes stirring. However, stirring does reduce cooking time by equalizing the temperature for sensitive foods that must cook more slowly. Stir foods from the outside of the dish toward the center. Heated portions are moved from the edges to the center; cool portions to the edges where they cook faster.

TURNING is a technique common to conventional and microwave cooking. This helps food heat evenly and in microwaving is done once during the cooking time of large, dense foods like this ham...or roasts or whole poultry.

ARRANGEMENT of unevenly-shaped food in the cooking dish is done to assure uniform cooking. Place thinner, less dense areas toward the center of the dish; thicker or more dense areas to the outside where microwave cooking begins first. Denser parts which take longer to cook receive more microwave energy and will be done at the same time as the less dense areas.

ARRANGEMENT when cooking several items of food at once in the oven is important, too. The potatoes illustrate the pattern that works best. The smaller potatoes are placed in the center with the larger around the outside where microwave cooking begins first. Other individual foods that should be arranged in a ring pattern include custard, individual meatloaves and several cups of coffee.

REARRANGEMENT is usually the same principle as stirring—moving food to help it cook more evenly. While stirring is common in both conventional and microwave cooking, rearrangement is a technique usually used only in microwave cooking. You'll use rearrangement for foods like meatballs or chicken pieces (foods that can't be stirred).

SHIELDING is done to slow down the cooking process in areas of food that appear dry or seem to be cooking too quickly. Small pieces of foil may be used to shield these areas in roasts, hams, turkey breasts, wings or legs. Microwaves bounce off the aluminum foil and prevent overcooking. Be sure you only shield delicate areas as foil in your oven in quantity may cause arcing that pits the oven interior. If arcing occurs, remove foil.

Microwave Techniques

In microwave cooking, as in conventional cooking, covering speeds cooking time, retains moisture, tenderizes, insures even cooking and prevents spattering. Different foods call for different covers and it's important to use the appropriate cover in each instance. Unless a recipe in this book specifies use of a cover, you can assume one shouldn't be used.

PLASTIC WRAP is a tight cover that helps hold in steam. This tenderizes and cooks foods quickly—especially vegetables and meats. Use plastic wrap when you don't have a glass lid that fits the utensil you're using. Plastic wrap may also be used to wrap some individual vegetables during cooking. And take care when removing the wrap—pierce it first to allow steam to escape.

GLASS COVERS fit tightly and help foods retain moisture and cook quickly and evenly. Use glass lids for vegetables, casseroles and some meats. Again, be careful removing the lid to avoid steam burns.

PLASTIC WRAP

GLASS COVERS

PAPER TOWELS AND NAPKINS

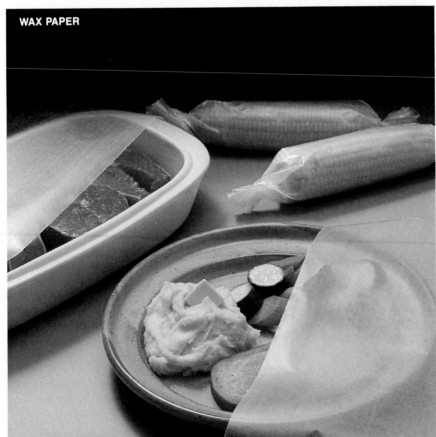

WAX PAPER

PAPER TOWELS AND NAPKINS
are loose covers used to prevent
spatters or to absorb moisture.
Wrap a sandwich or sweet roll in a
paper towel or napkin to absorb
moisture and prevent food from
becoming soggy. Cover bacon or
a plate of food with a paper towel
or napkin to prevent spatters in
your oven. **CAUTION:** Do not
place towels under baked
potatoes during cooking and
only cook bacon between paper
towels when cooking less than 4
slices. Some towels are made of
recycled materials that may
contain metal particles which can
cause fire when soaked with fat.

WAX PAPER is also a loose
covering which holds in some
heat for faster cooking of foods
that don't require steam to
tenderize. It also prevents
spattering in your oven. Use it
mainly for fish and poultry pieces,
but also for lasagna, some
casseroles and to wrap corn on
the cob during cooking.

19

Microwave Techniques

The utensil you cook in is almost as important as the food you cook in microwaving. Choosing the proper size and shape of the dish affects how the food cooks, the attention needed and the cooking time.

SIZE of cooking utensil and amount of food should match. Fill dishes half to two-thirds full. (This allows some leeway for bubbling.) If the dish is too small, food will bubble over the edges. And if the dish is too large, saucy portions of the food will spread out and overcook because more microwave energy reaches it. The bowl used for the candy · mixture in the photograph is three times larger than the quantity— this prevents any chance of boil-overs, since some candy mixtures need to boil up to 25 minutes.

SIZE

DEPTH

SHAPE

RING

DEPTH of the utensil is about as important as size. Here we show two casseroles that hold the same amount of food. The narrower, more compact casserole takes longer to microwave, while the shallow one exposes more of the food surface to microwave energy and therefore cooks faster. Be sure to check your recipe for the correct size because the cooking time will vary.

SHAPE, or square vs. round dishes, is also important. In sensitive foods such as baked goods, round shapes microwave more evenly than squares or rectangles because more microwave energy penetrates square corners, which causes overcooking in some instances.

RING-shaped utensils (not metal, however) are ideal for foods that can't be stirred during cooking to equalize temperature. Ring shapes allow microwaves to penetrate the food from the center as well as the sides, top and bottom. This works especially well for cakes, and bread pudding.

Doneness, Standing & Holding Times

Tests for doneness generally don't differ much between microwaved and conventionally-cooked foods. These two pages will review the similarities before we move to standing and holding times on the next two pages—some concepts that are important in microwave cooking.

THERMOMETERS

KNIFE

FISH

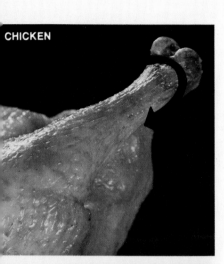

CHICKEN

TOOTHPICKS

MEAT

LOBSTER and shellfish microwave quickly and shouldn't be overcooked. They're done when the flesh loses its translucence and becomes opaque. Be careful not to overcook seafood or it will toughen. The shell of the lobster will turn bright red. Generally, 2 frozen lobster tails (about ¾ lb. each, thawed) should be microwaved **10 to 12 minutes** on **HIGH.** Then let stand, covered, 5 minutes before serving.

THERMOMETERS are a valuable aid in doneness testing. But only use those manufactured specifically for use in microwave ovens. Conventional meat and candy thermometers may be used outside the oven, but never during cooking. Probes and microwave thermometers measure the internal temperature of meat. A probe is connected to the oven and will shut off the oven when the internal temperature reaches a pre-designated limit. Be careful not to place your microwave meat thermometer near any bone or fat or the temperature will measure incorrectly. Use a meat thermometer in the thickest part of the thigh of whole poultry. But don't rely on this totally. Check How-To on turkey, page 64.

KNIFE tests are used for custard in both conventional and microwave cooking. Insert the knife halfway between the center and edge of the custard. Remove from oven if the knife comes out clean. The center will appear soft, but sets on standing. When cooking individual custards, check individually and remove as they finish cooking. Custards may cook at slightly different rates because the amount of custard in each cup tends to vary.

FISH is done if it flakes easily when lifted gently with a fork. The center will be slightly translucent, but will cook on standing. Be careful not to overcook fish or it will become dry and tough.

CHICKEN drumsticks move freely at the joints and meat cut near the bone is no longer pink when done. Check the bone areas in the breast and both thighs. Use a microwave meat thermometer in the thickest part of the thigh to check doneness in whole birds. (Insert it after the bird is turned.) Meat is done if the thermometer registers 180°F. when the bird comes from the oven. Pop-out indicators don't register accurately in microwave ovens, but may be left in the birds during cooking. Other doneness tests: Meat and juices are no longer pink when the bird is sliced between leg and body. Leg and thigh meat of small birds is tender when pinched.

TOOTHPICKS come in handy in microwave cooking as well as conventional cooking. Insert in center of cake and if it comes out clean, the cake is done. You may notice moist spots on the surface of cake, but these dry on standing. Do not insert the wooden toothpick into these moist spots, however.

MEAT is done when it's tender. Less tender cuts of meat will split at the fibers, so allow standing time to tenderize. Standing time is very important in meats. Use a food probe or thermometer to check for doneness. Internal temperatures will rise up to 15° F. during standing time, as the cut of meat finishes cooking. Of course, the final test of doneness is your own preference, as in conventional cooking.

Doneness, Standing & Holding Times

An important part of microwave cooking is standing time when many foods finish cooking outside the oven. Knowing the holding times of foods (length of time heat is retained) helps you in planning a microwave meal, too.

125°F

BEEF ROASTS

135°-140°F

HAMBURGERS

Some recipes will tell you to microwave to desired doneness. That means you check the food as you've always done—by opening the door periodically and tasting or visually checking it to see if it's done to your liking. But remember that **STANDING TIME** completes cooking on certain foods. So it is often advisable to undercook or underthaw food slightly in the oven to compensate. Standing time can take place anywhere— on the kitchen counter or in the oven with the power off. If the

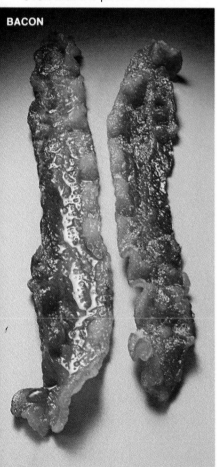

BACON

recipe says to let stand, covered … let the food stand with the same cover it had on during cooking. Allow roasts or poultry which are not covered during cooking to stand covered tightly with aluminum foil for about 10 to 20 minutes (depending on size) after being taken from oven.

For large **BEEF ROASTS** like the one shown here, internal temperature will rise up to 15°F. during standing time. The most accurate way to determine doneness of roast beef is with a microwave thermometer or probe which registers internal temperature.

Standing time is recommended whether you roast beef conventionally or in a microwave oven. This allows the juices to settle while the meat firms up for carving. And during this time the meat continues to cook. To avoid disappointment, remove the roast from the oven when the internal temperature is 10° to 15°F. lower than the finished temperature desired. If you roast beef to 135°F., often suggested for rare, the internal temperature will rise to 145°F. or 150°F. before serving … and that's medium. The suggested temperatures in the roast charts for rare, medium and well done are before standing time. Expect a 10° to 15°F. rise in temperature after standing.

HAMBURGERS should be allowed to stand, covered with foil for 1 to 2 minutes. During this time, the rare red color will turn brown, but the surface of the burger will not be crusty unless microwaved on the browning grill.

BACON should also be removed from the oven when it looks slightly underdone. It will be evenly cooked and brown after standing time.

HOLDING TIME and STANDING TIME are valuable tools in planning meals so that every food is ready to serve at the same time.

POTATOES, 4, for example, are heated through but are not done, and will feel firm, after 10 minutes of cooking time in the microwave. After standing another 5 minutes, the center is completely cooked. And when wrapped in foil after removal from the oven, potatoes will hold their heat up to 45 minutes, letting you prepare other foods that cool more quickly. (See pages 6 and 7 and 118 for care in not overcooking potatoes.) How long a food holds heat (when properly wrapped) depends on its size and density. Foods that hold heat for 20 to 45 minutes include ham, weighting over 4 lb., turkey, whole cauliflower, baked potatoes and whole sweet potatoes. Medium holding time foods (10 to 20 minutes) are chicken, meatloaf, most casseroles and cauliflowerets. Short (3 to 10 minutes) holding time foods: Fish fillets, hamburgers, peas, bread and cake.

A very good example of the holding time principle is **SQUASH** —whole vs. sliced squash. Here, standing times are about the same, but the larger whole squash will hold heat much longer than the smaller pieces.

Cooking food in the serving dish lengthens the time it will stay hot. Fish, casseroles and vegetables should be tightly covered. Large, whole vegetables should be wrapped in plastic or foil during standing and holding times. (Do not use foil during cooking time unless it's for shielding a small area.) Meats cooked in plastic bags or tightly covered dishes should be left covered during holding and standing times.

POTATOES

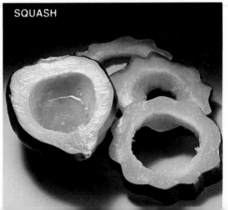

SQUASH

Browning Basics

Foods with high fat content or longer cooking times —roasts, bacon, whole chicken, turkey—brown on their own. Other foods don't. Use these steps for microwave browning of foods with low fat content and shorter cooking times.

A well around the outside of the browning grill surface catches fat and juices. Hamburger patties, steaks and chops are held above their juices and drippings on the grill surface where they brown evenly.

BROWNING GRILLS give you the capability for browning, searing, grilling and frying during microwave cooking. While you, your microwave oven and your kitchen all remain cool, you get the appeal of conventionally-broiled foods prepared with the speed of microwave.

The grill is made of a specially formulated ceramic material with a coating on the underside that absorbs microwave energy. Place the empty grill in the oven for preheating (times vary by food and brand of grill, so check manufacturers' recommendations). The microwaves are absorbed and the grill surface becomes very hot (500° to 600°F.). The handles will usually remain cool enough to touch, but with longer cooking times or when the well contains drippings it may be necessary to use hot pads for safe handling. When foods are placed on the grill, the hot surface begins the browning process. When the grill is returned to the oven, the food absorbs most of the microwaves, quickly cooking the interior while the browning continues on the outside of the food.

Foods on the grill are always cooked uncovered. Fats and juices may spatter when cooking meats, but they are easily wiped off the oven after cooking. Never cover the grill with paper towels, wax paper or plastic wrap to avoid spatters because they could catch fire due to the high degree of heat generated by the grill.

To prepare **GROUND BEEF PATTIES** on the browning grill, first mix 1½ lb. ground beef with all your favorite mouth-watering ingredients. Shape mixture into 6 patties. Preheat the browning grill as per manufacturers' instructions for ground beef patties. Place patties on the grill and microwave for **3 minutes** on **HIGH.** Then turn the patties over and continue cooking on **HIGH** for **2 to 3 minutes** or to desired doneness.

Of course there are other foods that won't brown in a microwave oven and that can't be prepared on a browning grill. **CAKE,** for example. But don't let that keep you from microwaving cakes. Frosting covers cake tops, so no one knows they're not as brown as when they're baked in conventional ovens. With cakes like pineapple upside down cake, the top ends up on the bottom, anyway. And then there are toppings you can add before or after baking. The crumb topping shown here, with cinnamon, sugar and nuts, is a delicious example.

Another example of a non-browning food is plain microwaved chicken. Here, if you wish, brush pieces with melted butter and sprinkle with paprika before microwaving for more color. Or use any of a number of delicious coating mixtures. (See suggestions on page 104.)

When preparing **HAM** or poultry, glaze with jelly, preserves, marmalade or other glazes that add both sheen and flavor to meat. For an orange glaze, combine ¼ cup orange juice, 2 tablespoons honey, 1 teaspoon grated orange rind and ½ teaspoon ginger. Mix well, pour over ham during the last 10 to 15 minutes of cooking time.

There are also a number of commercially-prepared browning agents on the market. These can be savory, sweet or unflavored. Some are applied full strength; most are diluted with water or butter. And all should be brushed on meats before microwaving. These include soy sauce, steak sauce, Worcestershire sauce and Kitchen Bouquet. Choose one that pleases your taste and corresponds with the food you're preparing.

Short Cuts With Your Microwave Oven

Here's a quick-reference chart you'll use every day.

Product	Quantity	Desired Result	Utensil	Setting & Time
Baby bottle	8 oz.	heat	Baby bottle; remove lid and nipple	REHEAT 1 to 1½ min. about 100°F.
Baby food	4 oz. jar	warm	Original jar (remove lid)	REHEAT 20 to 30 sec.
Bacon	4 slices	cook	12 x 7-inch glass baking dish	HIGH 4 to 6 min.
Bread, (frozen)	1 slice 1 loaf (1½ lb.)	defrost	Paper towel or napkin. Original plastic bag (remove twist-tie)	DEFROST (M. Low) 15 to 25 sec. DEFROST (M. Low) 1½ to 4 min.
Buns, Rolls (room temperature)	2	warm	Paper plate, paper towel or napkin	REHEAT 20 to 25 sec.
Butter (room temperature)	2 tablespoons ½ cup	melt soften melt soften	1-cup glass measure 1-cup glass measure 2-cup glass measure 2-cup glass measure	MED. HIGH (Roast) 45 sec. WARM 45 sec. to 1 min. MED. HIGH (Roast) 1½ to 2 min. WARM 1½ to 2½ min.
Cream cheese (refrigerated)	3 oz. 8 oz.	soften	Glass or pottery plate without metal trim (remove from foil pkg.)	WARM 2 to 2½ min. WARM 4 to 4½ min.
Chocolate chips	6 oz. pkg. 12 oz. pkg.	melt	2-cup glass measure 4-cup glass measure	HIGH 2 to 2½ min. (stir to blend) HIGH 2½ to 3 min. (stir to blend)
Chocolate	1 or 2 squares (1 oz. ea.)	melt	1-cup glass measure	HIGH about 1 to 2 min. (stir to blend)
Coffee, Tea	1 cup	reheat	Glass or pottery cup (without metal trim)	HIGH 1 to 2 min. about 160°F.
Casseroles (refrigerated)	1 serving 1 quart	reheat	Glass or pottery plate or bowl (without metal trim); cover with wax paper	REHEAT 3 to 4 min. REHEAT 10 to 14 min.
Hamburger (frozen)	1 lb.	defrost	Original plastic wrap	DEFROST (M. Low) 8 to 10 min.
Hot dogs (refrigerated)	2	heat	Wrap each loosely in paper towel or napkin	REHEAT 1 to 1½ min.
Juice (frozen concentrate)	6 oz. 12 oz.	defrost	Original container (remove lid)	DEFROST (M. Low) 2 to 2½ min. (let stand to complete defrosting) DEFROST (M. Low) 5 to 6 min. (let stand to complete defrosting)
Leftovers (refrigerated)	1 plate or bowl	reheat	Glass or pottery plate or bowl (without metal trim); cover with wax paper	REHEAT 4 to 5 min.
Meat	1 slice 1 platter	reheat	Glass or pottery plate or bowl (without metal trim); cover with wax paper	REHEAT 1 to 2 min. REHEAT 6 to 7 min.
Onion, Celery, Green peppers (chopped)	2 tablespoons 1 teaspoon butter ¼ cup 2 teaspoons butter ½ cup 1 tablespoon butter	saute	Glass mixing bowls or casseroles	HIGH 30 to 60 sec. HIGH 1 to 2 min. HIGH 2 to 3 min.
Pizza	1 to 2 slices	reheat	Paper plate, paper towel or napkin	MED. HIGH (Roast) 1 to 2 min.
Potatoes	4 medium	bake	(Pierce skin)	HIGH 10 to 15 min. (see pages 6 and 7 and 68 and 69)
Rice (cooked, refrigerated)	1 cup	reheat	Covered glass casserole	REHEAT 1½ to 2½ min.
Sandwich	1 2	reheat	Wrap in paper towel or napkin	REHEAT ½ to 1 min. REHEAT 1½ to 2 min.
Soup	2 bowls	heat	Glass or pottery serving bowls (without metal trim)	REHEAT 7 to 8 min. about 160°F.
Syrup, Sauces (refrigerated)	1 cup	warm	2-cup glass measure	REHEAT 2 to 3 min. about 150°F.
TV Dinner (frozen)	2 trays, 8 to 11 oz. each	heat	Original ¾-inch foil tray, uncovered, in paper cartons	REHEAT 14 to 16 min.
Vegetables	1 can (16 oz.), undrained	heat	1-quart covered glass casserole	REHEAT 3 to 5 min.

Dynamic Duo:
Your Microwave Oven and Conventional Appliances

Now your kitchen is complete! Use your microwave with conventional appliances for real efficiency. Start with one cooking method and finish with another, utilizing the best advantages of each for the maximum in speed and flavor.

The chart on the preceding page, the hints on this page and the easy-to-follow recipes on the following pages are just the beginning in dynamic duo ideas. You'll also want to start some foods in the microwave and finish in your conventional oven—foods like meat pies and yeast breads. Or, start beef stew and veal parmigiana on the range surface then finish fast in the microwave. Foods like roast duckling or any chicken recipe with sauce are fast, delicious and browned beautifully when started in the microwave and finished in your broiler. Here are even more ideas: **MELT BUTTER** or margarine for use in cooking. It's faster, easier and neater than the old-fashioned top-of-the-range technique. Melt

¼ cup butter from the refrigerator by placing in a 1-cup glass measure and microwaving on **MED. HIGH (Roast)** for **1 to 2 minutes.**

WARM SYRUP

MELT BUTTER

SOFTEN ICE CREAM

MELT CHOCOLATE in your microwave, too. Put one or two 1 oz. squares in a 1-cup glass measure and microwave on **HIGH** for **1 to 2 minutes.** Chocolate may not look melted, so stir to blend. Be careful not to overheat since chocolate burns very easily.
WARM SYRUP tastes better on hot pancakes (you can reheat leftover pancakes, too). So to heat 1 cup of syrup to about 150°F., pour into a 2-cup glass measure and microwave on **REHEAT** for **2 to 3 minutes.**
SOFTEN ICE CREAM, too. No more frozen fingers and bent spoons because now you can leave the ice cream in the carton, open the top and microwave on **WARM** for **1½ to 2½ minutes.** (For ½ gallon.)
SOFTEN CREAM CHEESE by removing the cheese from its original foil package, placing it on a glass or pottery plate (without metal trim), or in the mixing bowl to be used in your recipe, and microwaving on **WARM** for **4 to 4½ minutes.** (This is for 8 oz. cream cheese that has been refrigerated.)
PLUMP RAISINS and other dried fruits that aren't plump anymore. Place about 2 cups in a glass dish, sprinkle ¼ cup of water over them, cover with plastic wrap or a glass lid and microwave **2 to 3 minutes** on **HIGH.**

MELT CHOCOLATE

SOFTEN CREAM CHEESE

PLUMP RAISINS

Dynamic Duo:

Here are two examples of how your microwave oven can work with a conventional oven...and even your barbecue grill. You get delicious eating in half the time!

1 Preheat your conventional oven to 425°F. Prepare your favorite recipe for a 2-crust· fresh fruit pie. Assemble in a 9-inch glass pie plate.

2 Microwave for **7 to 10 minutes** on **HIGH,** or until juices start bubbling through slits in crust. (If you're preparing an unbaked, frozen pie, transfer it to a 9-inch glass pie plate and microwave for **13 to 16 minutes** on **HIGH.**)

The microwave oven isn't recommended for completely baking 2-crust pies (because the crust won't brown). But starting the baking process in your microwave oven gives the pie a head start toward doneness.

1 Place 2½ to 3 lb. of quartered frying chicken pieces skin-side-up and thick edges toward the outside in a 12 x 7-inch glass baking dish. Season with salt and pepper, if desired.

2 Place the chicken in the microwave oven for **15 to 18 minutes** on **HIGH.** You may hear "popping" noises as chicken is cooking, but don't worry, it's just the fat in the chicken rising to the surface. (Chicken will be slightly underdone after microwaving.)

Barbecued chicken fixed outdoors on the grill is unbeatable ...if your hungry family can wait. Here's how to speed up the process and still get that distinctive barbecue taste.

30

3 Transfer the pie to your preheated 425°F. conventional oven and bake 8 to 10 minutes, or until golden brown.

4 Now for the best part: You have a piping hot, golden brown, mouth-watering pie all set to eat. And it took you half the time it normally would.

3 Remove chicken from the oven and brush both sides of each chicken piece with your favorite barbecue sauce.

4 Now place the chicken over hot coals on the barbecue grill. Grill for 20 to 25 minutes; turn occasionally, and brush with barbecue sauce until chicken is fork-tender.

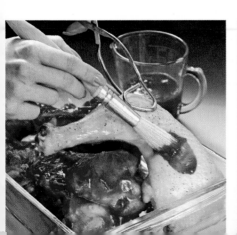

4 to 6 Servings
Use your microwave the next day to reheat any leftover chicken (see page 37).

Making Fast Foods Faster

Convenience foods have made all our lives easier for years. But since the advent of microwave ovens, convenience has never been so convenient.

Many convenience foods now contain microwave instructions along with conventional methods of preparation. We'd like to say follow these without hesitation, but this isn't always possible. Because microwave ovens differ by manufacturer, it's best when following these directions to start with the minimum cooking times given. Then, if more is needed, add time in small increments to avoid overcooking.

When we say convenience or fast foods, we mean anything from instant soup in a cup to TV dinners to baby food. The chart on pages 34 and 35 sum up how to microwave most of them. Generic names of products are general terms not protected by

MUGS

trademarks. Look for your favorite packaged foods under their common names. Let's talk about heating water for packaged mixes first. The water stays the same, but it's the amount and utensil used that makes the difference here. Take **MUGS,** for instance. To microwave one 8 oz. glass or pottery mug (without metal trim) of water to about 160°F., place on the bottom of your oven. Stir the water and microwave on **HIGH** for **1½ to 2 minutes.** Then you're all ready to prepare hot chocolate, instant coffee, tea, instant cup-of-soup or other delicacies. Two mugs of water will take **3 to 3½ minutes** on **HIGH** and 4 should be microwaved for **7 to 8 minutes.** Always remember to stir liquids when heating or reheating to prevent superheating.

GLASS MEASURES are used to heat water for instant mashed potatoes. Or in any of your microwave or conventional recipes where hot or boiling water is required.

GLASS BOWLS—serving or mixing bowls—can be put right in the microwave to boil water for gelatin or instant cereal such as quick-cooking oatmeal or grits.

CASSEROLE DISHES may also be used to heat water. Macaroni and cheese (the instant variety) is fast and easy. Just put 2 cups of water into a 2-quart glass casserole. Cover with glass lid or plastic wrap and microwave for **5 to 8 minutes** on **HIGH.** Then stir (7¼ oz.) pkg. mix into the boiling water and recover. Microwave for **10 to 12 minutes** on **MEDIUM (Simmer).** Let stand, covered, 3 minutes. Other possibilities include rice, noodles and instant scalloped potatoes.

GLASS MEASURES

GLASS BOWLS

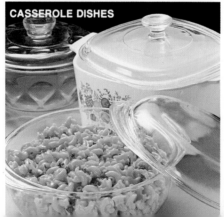

CASSEROLE DISHES

FROZEN CHICKEN becomes unfrozen, sizzling-hot and oh-so-good in your microwave oven in far less time than it takes in conventional ovens.

1 Arrange frozen, cooked chicken pieces (32 oz. pkg.) in a 12 x 7-inch glass baking dish. Make sure the thickest pieces are toward the outside of the dish.

2 Microwave for **10 to 15 minutes** on **REHEAT** or until hot. NOTE: It's all right to open the oven and check for doneness at any time, just as you would in your conventional oven.

3 Let the chicken stand for 3 minutes. Transfer to a platter and serve with your favorite microwaved vegetable. Chicken not all eaten? Serve it the next day for lunch.

For reheating 1 to 4 pieces of refrigerator-temperature chicken, see the Reheating Chart on page 37.

33

Making Fast Foods Faster

Food	Product and Size	Utensil	Setting and Time	Special Techniques
Beverages	Water/Milk 1 (8 oz.) 2 (8 oz. ea.) 4 (8 oz. ea.) 6 (8 oz. ea.)	Glass or pottery cups (without metal trim)	HIGH (about 160°F.) 1½ to 2 min. 3 to 3½ min. 7 to 8 min. 9 to 10 min.	Instant coffee or tea will fizz when stirred into hot liquid.
Cakes	Frozen 12 to 17 oz. 13 x 9 in.	Paper plate, towel or napkin	DEFROST (M. Low) 2 to 3 min. 3 to 4 min.	Remove from paper carton to thaw; stand 5 min.
Cookies/Bars	Brownies (etc.) Frosted (12 to 13 oz.) frozen	Original ¾-inch foil tray; remove lid	DEFROST (M. Low) 2 to 3 min.	Stand 5 min.
Fruits	Frozen 10 oz. 16 oz.	Original paper container; remove top or lid. Plastic pouch: slit & place in glass dish. Plastic bag: remove fruit and place in glass casserole, cover.	DEFROST (M. Low) 3 to 6 min. 7 to 10 min.	Fruit will remain icy in center; stir to loosen fruit.
Main Dishes	Chili with Beans (canned) 15 oz. 40 oz.	1-quart covered glass casserole	MED. HIGH (Roast) (about 150°F.) 5 to 7 min. 10 to 14 min.	Stand, covered, 3 min.
	Chow Mein 42 oz. beef, canned 24 oz. chicken, canned 32 oz. chicken, frozen	2-quart covered glass casserole 12 x 7-inch glass dish covered with wax paper	REHEAT (about 150°F.) 8 to 12 min. 7 to 9 min. 25 to 30 min.	Combine both cans and heat. Stand, covered, 3 min. Remove from foil tray if deeper than ¾-inch. Stand 3 min.
	Corned Beef Hash 15 oz., canned	1-quart glass casserole	REHEAT (about 150°F.) 5 to 7 min.	Stand 3 min.
	Hamburger Main Dish Mixes Macaroni or Noodle, (7 to 8 oz.) 1 lb. hamburger mix	2½-quart covered glass casserole	 HIGH about 5 min. HIGH 14-15 min.	Brown hamburger for HIGH time. Add dry mix envelopes, cover and cook on HIGH, stirring ½ way. Let stand, covered, 5 min. before serving.
	Lasagna 21 oz., frozen 50 oz., frozen	Remove from foil tray to 12 x 7-inch glass baking dish, covered	MED. HIGH (Roast) (about 150°F.) 20 to 25 min. 30 to 35 min.	Stand, covered, 5 min.
	Meat Pies 8 oz., frozen 2 pies 4 pies	Oven-proof glass or pottery plate (without metal trim)	HIGH 7 to 9 min. 8 to 11 min.	Brown in preheated 425°F. oven after thawing in microwave.
	Spaghetti 14 to 15 oz., canned 26 oz., canned	1-quart covered glass casserole 1½-quart covered glass casserole	REHEAT (about 150°F.) 3 to 4 min. 8 to 10 min.	Stand, covered, 3 min.
	Spaghetti Sauce 15½ oz., canned 32 oz., canned	1-quart covered glass casserole 1½-quart covered glass casserole	REHEAT (about 150°F.) 6 to 7 min. 8 to 10 min.	Stir once. Stand, covered, 3 min. Stir during heating.
	Tuna Main Dish Mixes Macaroni, noodle (7 to 9 oz.) or rice (8 to 9 oz.)	2½-quart covered glass casserole	HIGH 5 to 8 min. HIGH 8 to 10 min.	Combine tuna, liquid and mixes; boil on HIGH; stir; then HIGH until done. Stand, covered, 5 min.

Food	Product and Size	Utensil	Setting and Time	Special Techniques
	TV Dinners Meat with 2 to 3 other foods. 1 tray (8 to 11 oz.) 2 trays (8 to 11 oz. ea.) 1 tray (15 to 16 oz.) 2 trays (15 to 16 oz. ea.)	Foil tray, uncovered, in carton or covered with wax paper	REHEAT (about 150°F.) 8 to 10 min. 14 to 16 min. 10 to 12 min. 18 to 20 min.	Foil tray, should be no more than ¾-inch deep. Remove foil covers. Remove rolls or bread; return to tray during last 20 seconds of cooking. Stand, covered, 3 min.
	Meat Entrees with sensitive ingredients 2 trays (10 to 11 oz. ea.)		MED. HIGH (Roast) (about 150°F.) 12 to 14 min.	
Meat	Sausage, Pork Precooked links or patties (8 oz.) Frozen	Glass pie plate, cover with wax paper	REHEAT (about 120°F.) 3 to 4 min.	—
Pie	Pastry Shell 9 in. frozen	9-inch glass pie plate	MED. HIGH (Roast) 5 to 6 min.	Prick bottom and sides of shell.
Poultry	Turkey Roast 2 lb. frozen	9 x 5-inch glass loaf dish; cover	MED. HIGH (Roast) (about 175°F.) 38 to 42 min.	Turn over once halfway through cooking. Stand, covered, 5 min.
Sandwiches	Meat Sandwich— Hamburger (including fast food) 1, frozen 2, frozen 4, frozen	Wrap sandwiches in paper towel or napkin	REHEAT (about 140°F.) 2½ to 3 min. 3 to 4 min. 5 to 5½ min.	Use MED. HIGH (Roast) setting if sensitive ingredients included. Increase time a few seconds.
Seafood	Shrimp Cooked, 6 oz. frozen	1½-quart covered glass casserole	DEFROST (M. Low) 5 to 8 min.	Let stand, covered, 2 min.
Stews	Canned 16 oz. 40 oz.	1-quart covered glass casserole 2-quart covered glass casserole	REHEAT (about 150°F.) 4 to 6 min. 9 to 12 min.	Stand, covered, 3 min.
Vegetables	Au Gratin 11½ oz., frozen	9 x 5-inch loaf dish; cover with wax paper	MED. HIGH (Roast) (about 150°F.) 10 to 14 min.	Stand, covered, 3 min.
	Baked Beans 20 to 21 oz., canned	1½-quart covered glass casserole	MED. HIGH (Roast) (about 150°F.) 7 to 9 min.	Stand, covered, 3 min.
	Potatoes Baked, stuffed with sour cream, chives, cheese, frozen 1 pkg. (12 oz.)	1-quart covered glass casserole	MED. HIGH (Roast) (about 150°F.) 10 to 12 min.	—
	Instant Mashed 2 servings, water and salt 4 servings, water and salt	1-quart glass casserole	HIGH 2 to 3 min. 3 to 5 min.	Boil water and salt as pkg. directs—stir potatoes into boiling water.
	Scalloped 5 to 6 oz., dry mix 4 to 5 oz., dry mix with sour cream, etc.	3-quart covered glass casserole	REHEAT 18 to 21 min. MED. HIGH (Roast) 20 to 25 min.	Prepare as pkg. directs. Stand, covered, 3 min.

EEP FROZEN

Second Time Around

If leftovers have a bad name around your home, they won't anymore. You'll find out that reheating them in your new microwave makes them taste as good or better than they were the first time around.

1 To reheat a plate of food, arrange the plate with thick or denser foods toward the outside and the sensitive or quick-heating foods to the center of the plate. (Make sure the plate has no metal trim.)

2 Cover with wax paper to hold in heat and moisture. Microwave 1 refrigerator-temperature plate of food for **4 to 5 minutes** on **REHEAT** (A room-temperature plate will take **3 to 4 minutes** on **REHEAT**).

3 Let the plate of food stand covered about 3 minutes. Then remove the wax paper, serve and enjoy.

1 To reheat casseroles or main dishes, spread out in dish to an even depth for fast, uniform heating.

2 Always cover casseroles or main dishes with a glass lid or plastic wrap to hold in moisture and speed heating.

3 Microwave a 1-quart casserole of leftovers (refrigerator-temperature) for **10 to 14 minutes** on **REHEAT.** Stir if possible, halfway through the reheating time. Let casserole stand covered for 5 minutes before serving. (Reheat a 2-quart casserole of leftovers for **14 to 18 minutes** on **REHEAT.** Reheat 2 cups for **4 to 6 minutes** on **REHEAT.**)

Reheating Foods

Food	Product and Size	Utensil	Setting and Time	Special Techniques
Breads	Doughnuts (Cake or Raised), Sweet Rolls, Coffee Cake, Muffins	Paper plate, towel or napkin	REHEAT	Add about 5 sec. if frozen.
	1, room temp.		10 to 20 sec.	
	2, room temp.		20 to 30 sec.	
	4, room temp.		35 to 45 sec.	
	6, room temp.		45 to 50 sec.	
	Pancakes, French Toast, Waffles, English Muffins,	Paper plate, towel or napkin	REHEAT	Add 20 to 35 sec. if frozen.
	1, room temp.		10 to 25 sec.	
	2, room temp.		15 to 30 sec.	
	4, room temp.		25 to 40 sec.	
Meats	Hamburger Patties Cooked and frozen	Glass or pottery plate (without metal trim) cover with wax paper	REHEAT (about 150°F.)	
	1		1 to 2 min.	—
	2		1½ to 3½ min.	—
	6		5 to 7 min.	—
	Sliced Cooked Meat Frozen	Glass or pottery plate (without metal trim) cover with wax paper	REHEAT	Stand, covered, 2 min.
	1 slice		2 to 4 min.	
	4 slices		6 to 8 min.	
	Refrigerated			
	1 slice		1 to 2 min.	
	1 platter		6 to 7 min.	
Poultry	Chicken Precooked	Glass plate (without metal trim)	REHEAT (about 150°F.)	
	1 pc., refrig.		1 to 2 min.	—
	4 pcs., refrig.		2 to 3½ min.	—
Rice	Cooked	Covered glass casserole	REHEAT	Stand, covered, 2 min.
	1 cup, refrig.		1½ to 2½ min.	
	2 cups, refrig.		3 to 5 min.	
Sandwiches	Meat Sandwich— Hamburger (including fast food)	Wrap sandwiches in paper towel or napkin	REHEAT (about 140°F.)	Use MED. HIGH (Roast) setting if sensitive ingredients included. Increase time a few seconds.
	1, room temp.		25 to 30 sec.	
	1, refrig.		½ to 1 min.	
	2, room temp.		30 to 45 sec.	
	2, refrig.		1½ to 2 min.	
Soups	Refrigerated Tomato, Cream, Noodle or Vegetable	Glass or pottery bowls (without metal trim)	REHEAT (about 160°F.)	
	1 bowl		3½ to 4 min.	—
	2 bowls		7 to 8 min.	—
	Cream of Mushroom, Pea, Bean		MED. HIGH (Roast) (about 160°F.)	
	1 bowl		4 to 5 min.	—
	2 bowls		9 to 10 min.	—

Defrosting

Meal planning has just become easier. A whole chicken takes just an hour (including standing time) to defrost with your microwave! And remember, just because you've defrosted in the microwave doesn't mean you have to cook right away. You can refrigerate for later use, too. Here are some general defrosting guidelines:

Be sure to refer to your use and care manual for instructions for special defrost features.

● Thaw fish, seafood, meat or poultry in original, closed packages, if desired. ● Metal clips and pop-up timers may be left in poultry but remove metal twist-ties from bags and replace with a rubber band or string. ● Place food in a flat glass baking dish to catch drippings. ● Use **DEFROST (Med. Low)** setting to thaw: Fish and meat weighing up to 4 lb.; ground meat up to 2 lb.; poultry weighing 4 lb. or less. ● Use **HIGH/MED. HIGH (Roast)** to thaw: Large roasts 4 lb. and over; ground meat 2 lb. and over; poultry over 4 lb. ● Thaw **1 minute** per pound on **HIGH: 2 minutes** per pound on **MED. HIGH (Roast).** ● Food will be icy in the center when removed from oven. But edges begin cooking if microwaves thaw food totally.

GROUND BEEF is easiest to defrost when it's frozen in recipe-size amounts—1 or 2 pounds, for instance.

1 Place 1 (1 lb.) pkg. of frozen ground beef (remove original package) in 12 x 7-inch glass baking dish with or without microwave roasting rack. Place dish in oven and microwave **8 to 10 minutes** on **DEFROST (Med. Low).** (For defrosting larger amounts, see chart, page 40.)

2 Remove dish from oven. Ground beef will be icy in the center. (Edges will begin to cook if microwaves are allowed to thaw the meat completely.) Let stand 5 minutes to finish thawing.

3 If ground beef is to be cooked immediately (either by microwave or conventional methods), break apart with fork. If you've defrosted the meat for later use, be sure to refrigerate.

You may want to defrost **WHOLE CHICKEN** for use later on. If so, refrigerate after thawing. Otherwise proceed directly to cooking conventionally or in your microwave oven.

1 Place whole frying chicken (2 to 3 lb.) which is still in its original plastic bag in a 12 x 7-inch glass baking dish. Remove metal twist-tie from the plastic bag.

2 Replace metal twist-tie with a rubber band or string. Microwave **20 to 35 minutes** on **DEFROST (M. Low).**

3 Place chicken (in original closed plastic bag) in cold water for 30 minutes to 1 hour to complete thawing process.

4 Remove the chicken from plastic bag. Remove loosened giblets and rinse with cold water until center of chicken is no longer icy.

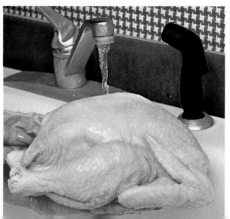

Defrosting Meat, Fish and Poultry

Here's a handy reference chart for defrosting. Where turning is specified, start defrosting whole poultry breast-side-up, and meats tray-side-up. This chart specifies standing time and standing techniques that will complete thawing. Refer to your use and care manual for specific timing for special defrost features.

	Cut and Weight	First Setting and Time	Second Setting and Time	Standing Time	Special Techniques
FISH	**FILLETS** 1 lb. pkg. 2 lb. pkg.	DEFROST (M. Low) 9 to 11 min. 14 to 20 min.	— —	10 to 15 min. 10 to 15 min.	Carefully separate and rinse under cold running water to finish thawing.
	WHOLE FISH 1½ to 2 lb.	DEFROST (M. Low) 18 to 25 min.	—	10 to 15 min.	See Fillets, above.
MEAT	**BEEF** **Ground Beef** 1 lb. 2 lb.	DEFROST (M. Low) 8 to 10 min. HIGH 1 min. per lb.	— MED. HIGH (Roast) 2 min. per lb.	10 to 15 min. 10 to 15 min.	— —
	Roasts 3 to 4 lb. 5 to 8 lb.	HIGH 1 min. per lb. 1 min. per lb.	MED. HIGH (Roast) 2 to 4 min. per lb. 2 to 4 min. per lb.	1 hr. 1½ hrs.	Shield ends with foil. Turn over once.
	Steaks Cubed, ½ lb. Rib-eye, 2 to 3 lb. Round or Sirloin 1½ to 2 lb.	DEFROST (M. Low) 3 to 4 min. 8 to 12 min. 12 to 17 min.	— — —	10 to 15 min. 10 to 15 min. 10 to 15 min.	— — Shield ends with foil.
	Stew Meat 1 to 2 lb.	DEFROST (M. Low) 8 to 12 min.	—	10 to 15 min.	—
	LAMB Ground or Patties 1 to 1½ lb.	DEFROST (M. Low) 6 to 10 min.	—	10 to 15 min.	—
	Roast, leg or shoulder 3 to 4½ lb.	HIGH 1 min. per lb.	MED. HIGH (Roast) 2 to 4 min. per lb.	1 to 1½ hrs.	Turn over once.
	PORK Bacon 1 lb.	DEFROST (M. Low) 6 to 7 min.	—	10 to 15 min.	—
	Chops ½ in. thick 1 to 1½ lb. 1 in. thick (loin) 3 to 3½ lb.	DEFROST (M. Low) 10 to 15 min. 12 to 20 min.	— —	10 to 15 min. 10 to 15 min.	— —
	Ground fresh or ham 1 lb.	DEFROST (M. Low) 8 to 10 min.	—	10 to 15 min.	—
	Ham 3 to 5 lb.	HIGH 1 min. per lb.	MED. HIGH (Roast) 2 to 4 min. per lb.	1 to 1½ hrs.	Turn over once.
	Roast 4 to 5 lb.	HIGH 1 min. per lb.	MED. HIGH (Roast) 2 to 4 min. per lb.	1 to 1½ hrs.	Turn over once.
	Sausage fresh ground 12 oz. bulk 1 lb. bulk links, precooked ½ lb. 12 oz. links, uncooked 1 lb.	DEFROST (M. Low) 5 to 7 min. 6 to 8 min. 3 to 5 min. 4 to 6 min. 4 to 6 min.	 — — — — —	 10 to 15 min. 10 to 15 min. 10 to 15 min. 10 to 15 min. 10 to 15 min.	 Shield ends with foil. — — — —
	Spareribs and Country Style Ribs 2 to 3 lb.	DEFROST (M. Low) 15 to 25 min.	—	10 to 15 min.	—

	Cut and Weight	First Setting and Time	Second Setting and Time	Standing Time	Special Techniques
—MEAT CONT'D	Wieners	DEFROST (M. Low)			
	½ lb.	2 to 5 min.	—	10 to 15 min.	—
	1 lb.	5 to 10 min.	—	10 to 15 min.	Shield ends with foil.
	VARIETY MEATS				
	Liver	DEFROST (M. Low)			
	8 oz.	5 to 7 min.	—	10 to 15 min.	—
	1 lb.	7 to 10 min.	—	10 to 15 min.	—
	VEAL				
	Chops	DEFROST (M. Low)			
	1 to 2 lb.	12 to 15 min.	—	10 to 15 min.	—
	Rump Roast	HIGH	MED. HIGH (Roast)		
	2½ to 3 lb.	1 min. per lb.	2 to 4 min. per lb.	30 min. to 1 hr.	
	4 to 6 lb.	1 min. per lb.	2 to 4 min. per lb.	1 to 1½ hrs.	Turn over once.
POULTRY	**CHICKEN**				
	Fryer, whole	DEFROST (M. Low)			Stand in original container in cold water.
	2 to 3 lb.	20 to 35 min.	—	30 min. to 1 hr.	
	Fryer, quarters		Break		Stand in original container in cold water.
	2½ to 3 lb.	14 to 20 min.	apart	30 min. to 1 hr.	
	Roasting, whole				Stand in original container in cold water.
	3 to 4 lb.	25 to 35 min.	—	30 min. to 1 hr.	
	Breasts 1½ to 2 lb.	15 to 20 min.	—	15 to 30 min.	—
	ROCK CORNISH GAME HEN				
	Whole	DEFROST (M. Low)			
	2 (1 lb. 2 oz. each)	15 to 25 min.	—	15 to 30 min.	Stand in original container in cold water.
	4 (1 lb. 2 oz. each)	20 to 30 min.		30 min.	
	TURKEY				
	Breast, bone-in	HIGH	MED. HIGH (Roast)		
	4 to 8 lb.	1 min. per lb.	2 to 4 min. per lb.	20 to 30 min.	—
	Whole	HIGH	MED. HIGH (Roast)		Stand in original container in cold water. Turn large birds over once during thawing.
	8 to 12 lb.	1 min. per lb.	2 min. per lb.	1 to 1½ hrs.	
	12 to 20 lb.	1 min. per lb.	2 min. per lb.	1½ to 2 hrs.	
SEA-FOOD	**LOBSTER**				
	Tails	DEFROST (M. Low)			
	(2) ½ to ¾ lb. each	8 to 9 min.	—	10 to 15 min.	See Fillets, p. 40.
	Scallops				
	Bay	DEFROST (M. Low)			
	12 oz. pkg.	5 to 8 min.	—	10 to 15 min.	See Fillets, p. 40.
	1 lb. pkg.	6 to 9 min.	—	10 to 15 min.	
	Shrimp	DEFROST (M. Low)			
	½ lb. pkg	6 to 9 min.	—	10 to 15 min.	See Fillets, p. 40.
	1 lb. pkg.	9 to 12 min.	—	10 to 15 min.	

Now You're Cooking!

Now for the best part. It's time for you and your microwave oven to create magic! To become more comfortable with the oven, try some of these fast and easy snacks. Then, move to the Breakfast, Lunch and Dinner sections where step-by-step instructions will teach you the basic principles of microwave cooking. Finally, there's a recipe section (alphabetized by category) much like you'll find in other microwave cookbooks.

You'll notice that microwave recipes give spans of cooking time—**2 to 2½ minutes,** for example. For best results, start with the minimum time. You can always microwave food longer, but you can't subtract time from overcooked food. Also, only cover foods when the recipe specifies it. And use the recommended cover.

CARAMEL APPLES

1 pkg. (14 oz.) caramels
2 tablespoons hot water
6 medium apples
6 wood sticks

1 Place unwrapped caramels in buttered, deep, medium glass mixing bowl; add water. Cover with wax paper Microwave for **3 minutes** on **MED. HIGH (Roast).**

2 Stir; recover caramels and continue cooking for about **2 minutes** on **MED. HIGH (Roast),** or until melted.

3 Skewer each apple with wooden stick. Dip in melted caramel mixture, turning to coat evenly. Place dipped apples on buttered cookie sheet or wax paper. (If caramel mixture thickens while dipping apples, return to oven and resoften, covered on **MED. HIGH (Roast).**

6 Apples

MUFFIN PIZZA

1 pkg. (14 oz.) English muffins
1¼ cups chili sauce
¾ cup Mozzarella cheese,
   shredded
Italian seasoning

Pizza Garnishes

Green pepper, sliced
Pepperoni, sliced
Green onion, bias cut
Mushrooms, sliced
Olives, sliced

1 Split English muffins in half. (Toast if desired.) Top each half with 1½ tablespoons chili sauce, about 1 tablespoon shredded cheese, a sprinkle of Italian seasoning and two of the Pizza Garnishes.

2 Arrange 2 pizzas on a paper towel in the oven. Microwave for **2 to 3 minutes** on **MED. HIGH (Roast)** or until cheese is melted.
12 Pizzas
Here are times for microwaving

more or less than 2 pizzas at a time: Microwave:
1 Muffin Pizza for **1½ to 2 minutes** on **MED. HIGH (Roast)**.
3 Muffin Pizzas **2½ to 4 minutes** on **MED. HIGH (Roast)**.
4 Muffin Pizzas **3½ to 5 minutes** on **MED. HIGH (Roast)**.)

─ MAKE-A-MEAL ─

Meatloaf, Baked Potatoes and Corn
For Ovens with Racks

For convenience, ovens with racks have been designed to allow you to microwave different foods at the same time. As with conventional cooking, check foods as they are cooking adding foods which take very little cooking time like rolls near the end and then removing foods as they get done. Make-a-Meal suggestions are given throughout this cookbook; in addition specific meal suggestions for your oven are listed in your Use & Care manual.

---

lace 1 can (12 oz.) corn in a glass ish. Cover with glass lid or plastic rap. Place on floor of oven.

Place meatloaf (recipe, page 66) in center of rack in the lower rack position. Wash and pierce 4 potatoes. Place two potatoes on each side of the meatloaf.

Microwave 35 to 45 minutes on **HIGH**, or until meatloaf is well done in center (about 140°F) and potatoes are tender.

Breakfast

It's the most important meal of the day, but it's also the easiest meal to slight…or even skip altogether. Now that you have your microwave oven, time is on your side in the morning, and you can prepare nutritious hearty foods…fast.

They're Incredible...

...and deliciously edible. They're eggs and they microwave beautifully in individual servings or egg dishes once you understand that the yolks cook faster than the whites. The hot water used in poaching eggs helps even the cooking of the egg yolk and the white and supplements microwave cooking.

Pictured: Scrambled Eggs page 45; Bacon, chart page 48.

Since eggs are a sensitive ingredient (see page 15), always microwave omelettes, scrambled eggs and other dishes with beaten egg mixture on **MED. HIGH (Roast)** to cook the center without overcooking outside edges. Be careful to cook eggs just until set or they'll toughen. Eggs finish cooking after they're taken from the oven.

When you scramble eggs, the whites and yolks are combined so the difference in cooking times are evened out. But we recommend frying or baking eggs in conventional ways, since microwaving may result in watery whites and hard yolks.

REMEMBER: DO NOT MICROWAVE eggs in the shell or reheat hard cooked eggs with or without the shell. Fat in yolks cooks quickly, builds up pressure and may explode, even when microwaved at a low setting.

Scrambled Eggs (number)	Milk (amount)	Butter (amount)	Microwave Setting & Time
1	1 tablespoon	1 teaspoon	*MED. HIGH (Roast) 1 to 1½ min.
2	2 tablespoons	2 teaspoons	*MED. HIGH (Roast) 2 to 2½ min.
4	4 tablespoons	4 teaspoons	*MED. HIGH (Roast) 4½ to 5 min.
6	6 tablespoons	2 tablespoons	*MED. HIGH (Roast) 7 to 7½ min.

*Stir half-way through cooking time

1 Combine 3 eggs and 3 tablespoons milk in greased soup bowl or 20-oz. glass casserole without metal trim (1-quart size for 4, 5 or 6 eggs). Beat together with fork or wire whisk.

2 Add 1 tablespoon butter and other seasonings to taste. (Mushrooms, chopped green pepper or onions.) Cover with glass lid or wax paper. Microwave for **2 minutes** on **MED. HIGH (Roast).**

3 Open the oven door. Eggs are beginning to set around the edges. Stir with fork to bring set parts to the center of the dish. Then close the door and microwave for **1 to 1½ minutes** on **MED. HIGH (Roast).**

4 Remove scrambled eggs from oven while they are still moist. Let stand covered for 2 minutes (1 to 4 minutes for 1 through 6 eggs). Eggs will continue to cook and set completely during standing time. Stir gently with fork before serving.

Breakfast

Fruit in a microwave oven? It's not only possible, but great tasting. Try these two for a delightful change of pace in the morning.

GLAZED GRAPEFRUIT
2 large grapefruit
3 tablespoons sugar
1 teaspoon cinnamon
2 teaspoons butter or margarine
4 to 5 teaspoons dry sherry or
orange juice
Mint leaves or cherries if desired

1 Cut grapefruit in half and cut around sections. Place each half in a glass serving bowl (without metal trim).

2 Combine sugar and cinnamon; sprinkle over grapefruit and dot with butter. Pour 1 teaspoon sherry over each half. Microwave for **6 to 7 minutes** on **HIGH,** or until warm.

3 Garnish with mint leaves or cherries and serve alone or as the beginning of a beautiful breakfast.
4 Servings
(For 2 halves, microwave **3 to 4 minutes** on **HIGH.** For 1 half, microwave **2 to 2½ minutes** on **HIGH.**)

OLD-FASHIONED BAKED APPLES

6 medium cooking apples, washed and cored
6 tablespoons brown sugar
3 tablespoons butter or margarine
½ teaspoon cinnamon

1 Make shallow cut in skin completely around each apple, one inch from the bottom. (To keep skin from shrinking during cooking.) Place apples in 12 x 7-inch glass baking dish (or 6 custard cups or serving bowls).

2 Place 1 tablespoon brown sugar and ½ tablespoon butter in center of each apple. Sprinkle with cinnamon.

3 Cover apples with wax paper. Microwave for **10 to 14 minutes** on **HIGH,** or until tender.

4 Let stand covered for 3 minutes before serving.
6 Servings
(For 1 apple, use individual custard cup or serving bowl and microwave for **2 to 3 minutes** on **HIGH,** 2 apples, use individual custard cups or serving bowls and microwave for **3 to 4 minutes on HIGH.**)

MAKE-A-MEAL
Add Scrambled Eggs

Prepare 4 Old-Fashioned Baked Apples through step 2 above. Cover with wax paper and place on rack in lower rack position. Prepare Scrambled Egg mixture using 6 eggs, recipe is on page 44. Cover with glass lid or wax paper. Place on floor of oven.
Microwave 7 minutes on **HIGH.** Stir the eggs; recover. Microwave 3 to 8 minutes on **HIGH** or until eggs are firm but still moist. Let stand 3 to 5 minutes before serving.

Breakfast

Breakfast isn't breakfast without bacon. Here are two ways to prepare it in the microwave: One method for 4 slices or more, the second method is for less.

BACON (4 or more slices)

1 Place 4 slices of bacon in a single layer in 12 x 7-inch glass baking dish...with or without a microwave roasting rack. (The roasting rack holds bacon above drippings.) Do not layer bacon between paper towels.

2 Cover bacon with paper towel to avoid spattering in your oven. Microwave **4 to 6 minutes** on **HIGH,** or until slightly underdone and almost crisp.

3 Let stand about 5 minutes to complete cooking and to crisp the bacon.

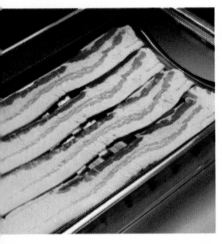

1 Layer 2 paper towels and place on glass, pottery or paper plate.

2 Place 2 slices of bacon on towels. Cover with another paper towel to avoid spatters in your oven. Paper towels will absorb grease. Microwave **2 to 3 minutes** on **HIGH,** or until bacon is slightly underdone.

3 Let stand about 1 minute to complete cooking and to crisp bacon.
NOTE: DO NOT use this method for 4 or more slices of bacon. And do not layer bacon between paper towels. This could result in fire.

Bacon	Utensil	Microwave Setting & Time
2 slices	Paper towel-lined glass, pottery or paper plate	HIGH 2 to 3 min.
4 slices	12 x 7 or	HIGH 4 to 6 min.
6 slices	13 x 9-inch glass	HIGH 5 to 8 min.
8 slices	baking dish, with or without microwave roasting rack	HIGH 6 to 10 min.

SAUSAGE PATTIES, using the browning grill, are a great way to greet the new day. Now you can do them in half the time it used to take in conventional cooking.

1 Preheat microwave browning grill (as per manufacturer's instructions for sausage patties). The special coating on the bottom will cause the grill to become hot enough to sear the patties, yet the handles will stay cool to the touch.

2 During preheat time, cut 12 oz. pkg. of sausage into 10 slices. Place slices on preheated grill. Microwave for **1½ minutes** on **HIGH.**

3 Turn the patties over and continue cooking for **2½ to 3½ minutes** on **HIGH,** or until done. You can expect some of the same smoking and spattering with the browning grill as in conventional broiling. But your oven wipes clean in a jiffy.

49

Breakfast

SAUSAGE LINKS, fresh or precooked, sizzle up great on your microwave browning grill. Be sure to check the manufacturer's instructions for correct preheat time.

1 Preheat microwave browning grill on **HIGH** for length of time manufacturer recommends for sausage links. Arrange 12 link sausages on preheated grill. Microwave for **1 minute** on **HIGH.**

2 Turn sausages over and continue cooking for **1½ minutes** on **HIGH.** Turn sausages again and cook for **1 to 2 minutes** on **HIGH,** or until done.

3 Serve immediately. (NOTE: If links are frozen, defrost them first, following instructions on pages 40 and 41.)

GRITS

1 cup grits
3 cups water
1 teaspoon salt
Butter
Salt and pepper

1 Place water and salt in large glass mixing bowl. Stir in grits. Cover with plastic wrap and microwave for **7 to 8 minutes** on **HIGH.**

2 Remove cover and stir. Recover and microwave another **4 to 4½ minutes** on **HIGH.**

3 Let stand 5 minutes. Serve with butter; salt and pepper to taste.
About 6 Servings

QUICK-COOKING OR INSTANT CEREAL
(oatmeal or grits)

1 Measure ¾ cup water, ¼ teaspoon salt and ⅓ cup cereal into individual serving bowl; mix well. Microwave for **2 to 3 minutes** on **HIGH.** (For 2 bowls, **2½ to 4½ minutes** on **HIGH;** for 4 bowls, **5½ to 7 minutes** on **HIGH.**

2 Stir cereal and let stand 1 to 2 minutes to complete cooking before serving.

3 Garnish and flavor each bowl of cooked cereal with 2 tablespoons of one of the following: Applesauce, brown sugar, jam, marmalade, honey, maple syrup or sprinkle with cinnamon and sugar.

51

Lunch

Super soup and sandwich lunches are what we look forward to all morning. You can microwave soups in glass casseroles, or glass or pottery serving bowls or mugs (without metal trim). Or measure and microwave instant soups right in a glass measure. Most sandwiches microwave easily on a paper towel or napkin, uncovered. Thick sandwiches should be wrapped loosely.

Pictured: Canned Tomato Soup, page 53.
Tomato/Bacon/Cheese Sandwiches, recipe page 54.

HEATING CANNED SOUP is easy. Follow directions on the can for adding milk or water. Most soups are cooked covered with fitted glass lids. Lift lids away from hands or arms to prevent steam burns. Plastic wrap may also be used to cover, but remember to pierce it before removing to allow steam to escape. Most soups are microwaved on **REHEAT.** But mushroom, bean or pea soup should be heated on **MED. HIGH (Roast)** to prevent "popping" (see page 15).

Soup	Setting	Minutes
DILUTED		
Broth 10½ oz.	**REHEAT**	3 to 5 (about 160°F.)
Tomato, Cream, Noodle, or Vegetable 10¾ oz.	**REHEAT**	5 to 7 (about 160°F.)
26 oz.	**REHEAT**	8 to 10 (about 160°F.)
Mushroom, Bean or Pea 10¾ oz.	**MED. HIGH (Roast)**	7 to 9 (about 160°F.)
UNDILUTED		
Chunk Vegetable, Noodle 10¾ oz.	**REHEAT**	2½ to 3½ (about 160°F.)
19 oz.	**REHEAT**	5 to 7 (about 160°F.)

1 Pour 1 can (10¾ oz.) tomato soup into 1½ or 2-quart glass casserole. Stir in milk or water as directed on can.

2 Cover soup with glass lid or plastic wrap. Microwave **5 to 7 minutes** on **REHEAT,** or until hot (about 160°F.).

3 Stir soup at end of cooking time with fork or wire whisk to blend. Let stand covered 2 to 3 minutes before serving.

4 Garnish hot soup with fresh parsley, lemon slices, croutons or other of your favorites.

Lunch

Now learn how to make all the basic sandwiches in your microwave oven.

TOMATO/BACON/CHEESE SANDWICH

8 tomato slices
8 slices bacon
4 slices cheese
4 green onions, sliced
4 bun halves, toasted, or 4 slices
 bread, toasted

1 Microwave the bacon following instructions on page 48. While bacon is standing, toast the bread or buns. Place 2 tomato slices on each half; add 2 slices bacon and top with 1 cheese slice and 1 sliced green onion.

2 Place 4 open-faced sandwiches on paper towels in the oven. Microwave for **3½ to 5 minutes on MED. HIGH (Roast),** or until sandwich is hot and cheese is melted. Since cheese is a sensitive ingredient, it may become tough and stringy if cooked too fast. Bread may also become tough if overcooked.

3 Garnish your sandwich with one or two of the following: Sliced green pepper, mushrooms, avocado slices, onion rings or sliced olives.
4 Sandwiches

MAKE-A-MEAL
Add Soup

Prepare sandwiches through Step 1. Place on paper towels, set aside. Pour 1 can (10¾ oz.) soup into 1½ or 2-quart glass casserole. Stir in milk or water as directed on can. Cover with glass lid or plastic wrap. Place soup on rack in upper rack position. Microwave soup 4 to 8 minutes; add sandwiches during the last 2 to 4 minutes of cooking.

HOT DOGS
2 wieners, refrigerated
2 hot dog buns

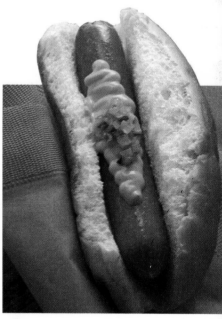

1 Place wieners in split hot dog buns; wrap each loosely in paper napkin or paper towel.

2 Place both hot dogs in oven and microwave for **1 to 1½ minutes** on **REHEAT.**

3 Garnish as desired with mustard, catsup or relish.
2 Hot dogs
(If using frozen or more than 6 wieners, do not put in bun, as increased cooking time will make bread tough. For 4 frozen wieners, place on paper or glass plate without metal trim, and microwave for about **4 to 5 minutes** on **HIGH** or until heated through.)

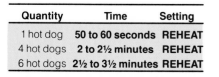

Quantity	Time	Setting
1 hot dog	50 to 60 seconds	REHEAT
4 hot dogs	2 to 2½ minutes	REHEAT
6 hot dogs	2½ to 3½ minutes	REHEAT

Lunch

Learning how to brown ground beef is a basic you'll use in all kinds of recipes. To do it, crumble it into a glass casserole and cover with a glass lid or plastic wrap. Microwave ½ lb. ground beef for **3 to 3½** **minutes** on **HIGH** in a 1-quart glass casserole. For 1½ lb. ground beef, use a 1½-quart glass casserole, covered, and microwave for **7 to 7½ minutes** on **HIGH.**

1 Crumble 1 lb. ground beef into 2-quart glass casserole. Stir in onion. Cover with glass lid.

2 Microwave for **5 to 6 minutes** on **HIGH;** drain fat. (Don't break apart chunks until after draining fat—it's easier to drain if you don't.)

SLOPPY JOE SANDWICHES
1 lb. ground beef
1 medium onion, chopped
1 cup bottled barbecue sauce
2 tablespoons packed brown
  sugar
1 teaspoon prepared mustard
6 hamburger buns, warmed

1 Place butter and onion in 2-quart glass casserole. Microwave for about **3 minutes** on **MED. HIGH (Roast),** or until onion is partly cooked.

2 Stir in remaining ingredients. Cover with glass lid or plastic wrap. Microwave for **4 minutes** on **MED. HIGH (Roast).**

MACARONI AND CHEESE
2 tablespoons butter or margarine
¼ cup finely chopped onion
2 cups shredded process
  American cheese
¾ cup milk
1 teaspoon salt
⅛ teaspoon pepper
4 cups cooked elbow macaroni

3 Stir in remaining ingredients for hamburger mixture; recover. Microwave for **5 to 6 minutes** on **REHEAT,** or until hot. Let stand, covered, 5 minutes before serving.

4 Spoon into warm, split hamburger buns. (You can warm them in your microwave, following instructions on page 28.)
6 Sandwiches

3 Stir lightly; recover, and continue cooking for **4 to 5 minutes** on **MED. HIGH (Roast),** or until piping hot. Let stand covered, 5 minutes before serving.

4 Garnishes you might want to consider include parsley, bacon bits, green onions and mushrooms. (This dish is just as good the next day when you reheat it in your microwave oven. See page 37 for instructions.)
4 to 6 Servings

Lunch

Whether company is coming or you just want an extra special lunch for yourself, these vegetable recipes are perfect. Fresh, microwaved vegetables are steam-cooked and so tender-crisp—firm to the touch when removed from the oven. Then standing time finishes cooking. Microwave cooking, plus a minimum of water, preserve the water-soluble vitamin content of vegetables.

SPICY-TOPPED TOMATOES

4 medium tomatoes
½ cup mayonnaise or salad
   dressing
2 green onions, sliced
1 tablespoon prepared mustard
½ teaspoon salt
⅛ teaspoon basil leaves
2 tablespoons crushed,
   unsweetened cereal flakes

1 Slice each tomato in half; arrange in bottom of 13 x 9-inch glass baking dish. Combine remaining ingredients except cereal flakes in small bowl.

2 Spread about 1½ tablespoons of the mixture on each tomato half; sprinkle with crushed cereal flakes. Microwave for **4 to 6 minutes** on **MED. HIGH (Roast)**, or until tomatoes are tender.

3 Let stand 2 minutes before serving.
4 to 6 Servings
(You used the **MED. HIGH (Roast)** setting in this recipe because mayonnaise and salad dressing are sensitive ingredients, see page 15.)

MICROWAVING CANNED VEGETABLES

All canned vegetables heat the same in a microwave oven. The only difference is whether you heat them drained or undrained. Drained vegetables take less time. Here's a chart showing times and setting.

Canned Vegetables (all kinds)	Microwave Setting & Time Undrained	Microwave Setting & Time Drained
	(to about 150°F.)	
8 oz.	REHEAT 2 to 2½ min.	REHEAT 1½ to 2 min.
15 oz.	REHEAT 3 to 4 min.	REHEAT 2½ to 3 min.
17 oz.	REHEAT 4 to 5 min.	REHEAT 3 to 3½ min.

FRENCH STYLE GREEN BEANS

1 Empty 1 can (15 oz.) French style green beans, undrained, into 1-quart glass casserole.

2 Cover with glass lid or plastic wrap. Microwave for **3 to 4 minutes** on **REHEAT,** or until hot (about 150°F.).

3 Let stand covered, 2 to 3 minutes to heat completely through. Garnish with bacon bits or French-fried onion rings.

Lunch

No lunch is complete without something sweet. Here are two especially good examples for lunch...or most anytime the sweet tooth calls for satisfaction.

**1** Place butter in 12 x 7-inch glass baking dish. Microwave for about **1 to 1½ minutes** on **MED. HIGH (Roast),** or until melted. Stir in marshmallows. Microwave for **1 minute** on **MED. HIGH (Roast).**

2 Stir and continue cooking for about **1½ to 2 minutes** on **MED. HIGH (Roast),** or until marshmallows are softened. Stir until smooth.

KRISPIE MARSHMALLOW TREATS
½ cup butter or margarine
5 cups miniature or 40 large marshmallows
5 cups crispy rice cereal

1 Measure 2 cups milk in 4-cup glass measure. Add 1 pkg. (3⅝ oz.) chocolate pudding mix.

2 Beat mixture well with rotary beater. Microwave for **4 minutes** on **HIGH.**

PUDDING AND PIE FILLING
Be sure to use a large enough utensil to avoid boil-overs.

Pudding & Pie Filling Mix	Glass Utensil	Microwave Setting & Time
4 Servings (3⅝ oz. pkg.)	4-cup measure	HIGH 6 to 7 min.
6 Servings (5½ oz. pkg.)	1½-quart casserole	HIGH 8 to 11 min.

3 Mix in cereal. Press into baking dish. Cool until set. Cut into squares.
24 to 30 Krispie Squares
(For Mint Chocolate Krispie Treats, add 1 pkg. (6 oz.) "real"

chocolate pieces to butter. Microwave for about **2 minutes** on **MED. HIGH (Roast),** or until melted. Stir ¼ to ½ teaspoon peppermint extract into melted marshmallows. Increase cereal to 6 cups.)

3 Again, beat mixture well with rotary beater. Microwave for **2 to 3 minutes** on **HIGH,** or until mixture boils and thickens.

4 If necessary, beat again lightly. Pour into serving dishes and chill to set. Top with whipped cream and chocolate curls, if desired.

Dinner

Your microwave oven is ideal for more than short cuts and reheating. It can help make dinner a very special occasion every night, too. Its speed and convenience make whole meals possible in a fraction of the time it would take with conventional cooking methods. Try complete meals cooked in a clay pot, or a turkey, or a rolled rib roast ...

Pictured: Country Pot Roast, recipe page 63.

CLAY POTS have been used for cooking throughout history, and they work especially well in microwave ovens. Because it's porous, the pot absorbs water when soaked before each use. (Soak according to manufacturer's instructions.) The water is then slowly released while cooking to make inexpensive cuts of meat really tender—but with microwave speed. In addition to tenderizing tough cuts of meat, you'll find the clay pot makes food taste better than ever because it blends and releases all the locked-in flavors of food.

And best yet, when the food is ready, the clay pot can go right to the table as an attractive serving dish. It retains heat while you savor your food...and then lets you enjoy hot second helpings, too.

Try your own favorite recipes in the clay pot...or try this one for Country Pot Roast. The roasts given in the chart are all less tender cuts. These should be microwaved using the clay pot method for pot roast.

REMEMBER: When using the clay pot, only microwave fresh or completely thawed meat. And always place meat fat-side-down for the first time setting. It's best not to add much liquid, if any, to most roasts. This is due to the large amounts of moisture in the clay pot itself. Too much liquid actually lengthens cooking time and toughens the meat.

Less-Tender Roasts	Utensil	First Setting & Time	Second Setting & Time	Special Techniques
Beef Chuck (2 to 4 lb.)	Soaked clay pot with lid	**HIGH, 5 min. per lb.**	**MEDIUM (Simmer), 15 min. per lb.**	Turn over once, halfway through cooking time.
Beef Rump, boneless or bone-in (3 to 4 lb.)	Soaked clay pot with lid	**HIGH, 5 min. per lb.**	**MEDIUM (Simmer), 25 min. per lb.**	Turn over once, halfway through cooking time.
Beef Sirloin Tip (4 to 5 lb.)	Soaked clay pot with lid	**HIGH, 5 min. per lb.**	**MEDIUM (Simmer), 20 min. per lb.**	Turn over once, halfway through cooking time.

COUNTRY POT ROAST

1 Soak both clay pot and lid in cold tap water (as per manufacturer's instructions). Completely drain the water from clay pot and lid, but do not dry.

2 Place 2½ to 3 lb. beef chuck roast in water-soaked clay pot. Sprinkle with your own, or with the following seasonings: 1 tablespoon dried parsley flakes, 1 tablespoon Worcestershire sauce, ½ teaspoon garlic salt and ¼ teaspoon pepper. Cover with water-soaked lid.

3 Microwave **15 minutes** on **HIGH.** Turn roast over for uniform cooking. During cooking, only remove lid when absolutely necessary. Frequent peeking releases steam and results in a less tender product and longer cooking time.

4 Add the following vegetables: 2 medium onions, quartered; 2 stalks celery, cut into chunks; 3 carrots, peeled and cut into chunks; and 6 to 8 small red potatoes. Recover, and microwave for **50 to 55 minutes** on **MEDIUM (Simmer),** or until meat and vegetables are tender. Let stand, covered, 5 minutes before serving.

About 4 Servings

Dinner

TALKING ABOUT TURKEY isn't as much fun as eating turkey prepared in your microwave. It's juicier and more tender than birds roasted conventionally. But before trying one, you should know that 14 lb. is the maximum size for a bird in the microwave. Also, microwave cooking times may increase up to 15 minutes when larger birds are stuffed.

1 Completely thaw and wash about a 10 lb. turkey (use technique on page 39 and check times on pages 40 and 41). (If turkey has a pop-out "doneness indicator," it may be left in but it will not be accurate.) Secure openings with toothpicks or metal skewers. Use string to tie legs together and wings to body. Season, if desired. Place turkey, breast-side-down, on microwave roasting rack in 12 x 7 or 13 x 9-inch glass baking dish. Microwave **6 minutes per lb.** or **60 minutes** on **HIGH.** (The "popping" you may hear is just fat being drawn to turkey's surface.)

2 Shield any areas on turkey which may be cooking too quickly (wings or drumsticks) with small pieces of foil. But do not allow foil to touch oven walls. Turn bird breast-side-up and microwave for **4 to 6 minutes per lb.** or **40 minutes** on **MED. HIGH (Roast),** or until done. Turkey is done if meat thermometer inserted in the thickest part of both thighs and breast registers 180°F. when the bird is taken from oven.

3 Let turkey stand 10 to 15 minutes, covered tightly with foil, before carving. During standing time, internal temperature will rise 10° to 15°F. Standing time completes cooking and sets juices to make carving easier.
(Turkey skin will not be crisp after microwaving. For crisp skin, place turkey under a 450°F. conventional oven broiler for 10 to 15 minutes before standing time.)

TENDER ROASTS are microwaved uncovered, on a microwave roasting rack. The times given in the meat chart on pages 90 and 91 are for fresh or completely thawed tender roasts. Microwave either by time or temperature with a microwave meat thermometer.

ROLLED RIB ROAST

1 Place fresh or thawed 4 lb. beef rolled rib roast, fat-side-down, on microwave roasting rack in a 12 x 7-inch glass baking dish. Season if desired.

2 Microwave **6 minutes per lb., on HIGH.** Turn roast fat-side-up and continue microwaving for **4 to 7 minutes** per lb. for Medium (about 145°F.) on **MED. HIGH (Roast).** Cook either by time to desired doneness, or use a microwave meat thermometer after roast is turned. (Do not use a conventional meat thermometer in the microwave. See pages 8 and 9.) For accuracy, make sure thermometer is inserted into the center of roast and not near any fat.

3 Let roast stand 10 minutes, covered tightly with foil to complete cooking and set juices before carving. During standing time, the internal temperature of the roast will rise up to 15°F. Temperatures given in Step 2 are temperatures before standing time.

4 Roast is microwaved to perfection, browned naturally as if it were done in your conventional oven... but in half the time. It browned on its own because of the relatively high fat content. And that also caused the "popping" noise you may have heard during cooking.

MAKE-A-MEAL
Add Baked Potatoes
Wash and pierce 6 potatoes. Prepare rolled rib roast through step 1. Place roast (about 4 lbs.) and potatoes on floor of oven. Microwave as directed under Rolled Rib Roast recipe this page, adding **10 to 20 minutes** additional cooking time. Let stand covered 10 minutes before serving.

Dinner

While you may want to improvise on these recipes for meatloaf and meatballs, these are the basic steps to follow when microwaving.

MEATLOAF

1 Combine the following ingredients in a medium mixing bowl: 1½ lb. ground beef; 2 cups soft bread cubes; ½ cup celery, finely chopped; ½ cup chopped onion; ¼ cup chopped green pepper; 1½ teaspoons salt; 1 egg and ½ cup catsup. Mix well and pat evenly into 9 x 5-inch glass loaf dish.

2 Brush meatloaf with a mixture of ½ cup catsup, ¼ cup chili sauce, 2 tablespoons brown sugar, 1 tablespoon lemon juice, 1 teaspoon dry mustard and 1 teaspoon Worcestershire sauce. Or, brush with catsup or barbecue sauce alone.

3 Microwave for **25 to 35 minutes** on **MED. HIGH (Roast),** or until well done in center (about 140°F). Pour off liquid and let stand, covered with foil for 5 minutes before serving.

MEATBALLS

They're a favorite served plain. And so good "fancied up" with our sweet and sour sauce.

1 Combine all meatball ingredients in a medium mixing bowl: 1 lb. ground beef; ¼ cup chopped onion; 1 egg, beaten; 1 teaspoon salt; ¼ teaspoon pepper and 2 tablespoons water. Mix well. Shape into 20 (1-inch) meatballs.

2 Place meatballs in 9-inch round glass baking dish. Cover with wax paper. Microwave for **8 to 9 minutes** on **MED. HIGH (Roast)** if adding sauce. (For meatballs alone, microwave for **8 to 11 minutes** on **MED. HIGH (Roast).)** Drain and let stand covered about 3 minutes.

3 During standing time for meatballs microwave sweet/sour sauce by placing 1 tablespoon butter or margarine and 1 small onion, chopped, in 1-quart glass casserole. Microwave for about **2 minutes** on **HIGH,** or until onion is partly cooked. Stir in 1 cup

4 Remove meatloaf from glass baking dish and serve.
Garnishes: During standing [ti]me, microwave several strips of [b]acon (see page 48) and place [o]n top. Or simply garnish with [fr]esh parsley.
[4] to 6 Servings

┌─ **MAKE-A-MEAL** ─┐
Add Baked Potatoes and Canned Vegetable
MAKE-A-MEAL by adding 4 Baked Potatoes and 1 can (12 oz.) corn to the Meatloaf. Follow the directions on page 43.
└────────────────┘

FISH FILLETS with Lemon Butter Sauce (or plain)
2 lb. frozen fish fillets, thawed
Lemon Butter Sauce
⅓ cup butter or margarine
⅓ cup slivered almonds
1 tablespoon dried parsley flakes
1 teaspoon lemon juice

1 Arrange fish fillets in 12 x 7-inch glass baking dish with thick edges toward outside of dish.

2 Cover with wax paper. Microwave for **8 to 12 minutes** on **HIGH.**

3 Drain liquid and let stand, covered, for 5 minutes to complete cooking.

4 During standing time, microwave sauce as follows: Place all ingredients in 2-cup glass measure. Microwave about **2 minutes** on **HIGH,** or until butter is melted. Stir and continue cooking **1 to 1½ minutes** on **HIGH,** or until lightly browned. Serve over fillets.
4 to 6 Servings

[k]atsup, 1½ tablespoons packed [b]rown sugar, 1½ tablespoons [le]mon juice and 1 tablespoon soy [s]auce. Pour sauce over meatballs [a]nd continue cooking for **3 to 5 [m]inutes** on **MED. HIGH (Roast),** [o]r until hot.

[2]0 Meatballs

Dinner

After tasting corn on the cob, baked potatoes and even frozen vegetables prepared in your microwave, you'll never be satisfied with conventionally-prepared vegetables again!

CORN ON THE COB

1 Husk, wash and trim 4 ears of corn. Place cobs in 12 x 7-inch glass baking dish. Do not add any water; it's not necessary.

2 Cover dish of corn with plastic wrap and place in oven. Microwave **7 to 10 minutes** on **HIGH.** (For 2 ears microwave **4 to 6 minutes** on **HIGH** and 6 ears **9 to 12 minutes** on **HIGH.** For frozen corn microwave 2 ears **6 to 10 minutes** on **HIGH** and 4 ears **10 to 14 minutes** on **HIGH.)**

3 To microwave individual ears of corn, wash and wrap each ear in plastic wrap; or pull husk back enough to remove silk from corn and wash. Rewrap husk around corn and cook directly on oven's bottom shelf.

FROZEN BRUSSELS SPROUTS
(Package or Pouch)

1 Place 1 (8 oz.) pkg. frozen brussels sprouts, icy-side-up, in 1½-quart glass casserole. Do not add water. Cover with glass lid or plastic wrap. Microwave **4 minutes** on **HIGH.** (Microwave ½ lb. fresh brussel sprouts **5 to 7 minutes** on **HIGH** and 1 lb. **7 to 8 minutes** on **HIGH.**)

2 Remove cover and stir brussels sprouts to equalize temperature and hasten cooking. Recover and continue cooking for **2 to 3 minutes** on **HIGH,** or until vegetables are tender-crisp.

3 To microwave a 10 oz. pouch of frozen brussels sprouts, slit the center of the pouch and place directly on the oven's bottom shelf. Microwave **6 to 7 minutes** on **HIGH,** or until tender-crisp. No need to stir or use a dish.

Corn may seem firm when removed from oven after microwaving. But cooking continues, so allow it to stand covered 2 to 5 minutes, depending on the number of ears being cooked. Season as desired.

4 Let both the casserole or pouch of brussels sprouts stand covered for about 3 minutes to complete cooking. Then serve. (Remember to open the pouch carefully to allow steam to escape.)

BAKED POTATOES

Bake potatoes in minutes instead of hours. Because potatoes have a high moisture content and a natural covering to hold steam inside during cooking, they cook quickly. And they're one of the best microwaved vegetables.

1 Wash and scrub thoroughly 4 medium baking potatoes.
IMPORTANT: Pierce or prick skins of potatoes with fork before cooking. This allows some steam to escape during cooking.

2 Place potatoes directly on the bottom shelf of the oven, in glass dish or on microwave roasting rack. Space at least 1 inch apart so that microwave energy can penetrate from all sides for even cooking. Microwave for **10 to 15 minutes** on **HIGH.**
CAUTION: Cooking as little as 10% more than suggested times may lead to overcooking. Old, dehydrated potatoes and small potatoes can overcook very quickly. Overcooking can lead to smoke and may possibly cause fire. NEVER LEAVE POTATOES UNATTENDED DURING COOKING. (See pages 6 and 7.) The "popping" noise is steam escaping through the tiny holes in the potatoes.

3 Potatoes will feel firm when squeezed. Take from oven, wrap in aluminum foil or place in a casserole dish; let stand for 5 minutes to complete cooking. (For microwaving different sizes or quantities see chart on page 118.)

4 Potatoes will hold their heat for up to 45 minutes. This long holding time frees your oven to prepare the rest of your meal. Serve baked potatoes with sour cream or butter (or both) and garnish with chives or bacon bits.

Dinner

1 Place 2 tablespoons butter or margarine in 1-cup glass measure. Microwave about **1 minute** on **MED. HIGH (Roast).** Stir in dry bread crumbs. Set aside.

2 Combine all ingredients (except buttered crumbs) in 1½-quart glass casserole. Microwave **9 minutes** on **HIGH.**

SCALLOPED POTATOES

1½ cups Basic White Sauce (page 113)
½ teaspoon salt
4 medium potatoes, peeled and thinly sliced
2 tablespoons butter or margarine
¼ cup dry bread crumbs

NOODLE CASSEROLE

(Ham, Pork, Tuna, Chicken or Turkey)
3 cups uncooked egg noodles
1 tablespoon butter or margarine
¼ cup chopped onion
½ cup chopped celery
1 can (10¾ oz.) condensed cream of mushroom soup
½ cup mayonnaise or salad dressing
1 can (6½ oz.) tuna, rinsed, drained and flaked, or 2 cups cubed, cooked ham, pork, chicken or turkey
¼ cup sunflower nuts
¼ cup crushed potato chips

1 Bring 4 cups water, 1 tablespoon cooking oil and 1 teaspoon salt to a full rolling boil in a 3-quart covered (glass lid or plastic wrap) glass casserole for **6 to 10 minutes** on **HIGH.** Stir in noodles and recover. Microwave **8 to 10 minutes** on **MEDIUM (Simmer),** or until tender. Drain, rinse with hot water and set aside.

2 Place butter, onion and celery in 2-quart glass casserole. Microwave about **3 minutes** on **HIGH,** or until partly cooked.

3 Stir potato mixture to equalize temperature and sprinkle with bread crumbs. Continue microwaving **9 to 11 minutes** on **HIGH,** or until potatoes are tender. Let stand 2 minutes.
About 4 Servings

Try Au Gratin potatoes using the same technique. Substitute 1½

cups Cheese Sauce (page 113) for white sauce in basic recipe. Microwave for **12 minutes** on **MED. HIGH (Roast).** Stir; sprinkle with buttered bread crumbs and continue cooking **13 to 16 minutes** on **MED. HIGH (Roast),** or until potatoes are tender. Let stand 2 minutes.
About 4 Servings

3 Stir in remaining ingredients (except potato chips). Sprinkle with crushed potato chips and microwave about **8 to 11 minutes** on **MED. HIGH (Roast),** or until heated through (about 150°F.).

4 Let stand 5 minutes before serving.
About 4 Servings

Appetizers & Beverages

Most appetizers and dips microwave on **MED. HIGH (Roast)** because they contain cheese, mayonnaise, mushrooms or cream cheese that need to cook gently. Most others with non-sensitive ingredients can be microwaved on **HIGH.** But experiment with one before doing a whole batch. Then add delicious hot beverages like the two on these pages...and you've got a party!

HOT FRUIT PUNCH

1 jar (32 oz.) cranberry juice
   cocktail
3 cups water
1 can (6 oz.) frozen orange juice
   concentrate, thawed
1 pkg. (10 oz.) frozen red
   raspberries, thawed
2 oranges, sliced
6 sticks cinnamon
12 whole allspice
½ to ¾ cup light rum or water

1 Combine all ingredients in 4-quart glass bowl or heat-resistant glass punch bowl.

2 Microwave **12 to 16 minutes,** on **HIGH,** or until hot (about 160°F.).

25 to 30 (4 oz.) Punch Cups

CREATE-A-HOT-DIP

1 pkg. (8 oz.) cream cheese
½ cup mayonnaise or salad
   dressing
2 green onions, sliced
1 tablespoon dried parsley flakes

1 Place cream cheese in medium glass mixing bowl.

2 Microwave about **2 to 2½ minutes** on **MED. HIGH (Roast),** or until softened. Add mayonnaise, onions, parsley **plus ingredients from one of the variations.**

RECIPE VARIATIONS

HOT CRAB DIP
Add 1 can (6 oz.) crabmeat, drained and flaked; ½ cup slivered almonds; 2 tablespoons dry white wine; 1 tablespoon horseradish and ¼ teaspoon Worcestershire sauce. Microwave **4 to 6 minutes** on **MED. HIGH (Roast),** or until hot (about 120°F.).

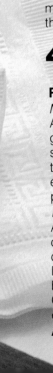

Pictured Clockwise: Hot Fruit Punch, Create-A-Hot-Dip, Munch Mix, Stuffed Mushrooms and Hot Spiced Cider.

HOT SPINACH DIP

Add 1 pkg. (10 oz.) frozen chopped spinach, thawed and drained well; 6 slices bacon, crisply fried and crumbled; ⅓ cup grated Parmesan cheese and 2 teaspoons lemon juice. Microwave **3 to 5 minutes** on **MED. HIGH (Roast),** or until hot (about 120°F.).
About 2 Cups Dip

STUFFED MUSHROOMS

1 lb. large fresh mushrooms
3 green onions, sliced
1 tablespoon butter or margarine
¼ cup sour cream
1 pkg. (8 oz.) cream cheese

1 Wash mushrooms; remove stem from each cap by twisting. Arrange caps, stem-side-up, in 13 x 9-inch glass baking dish; set aside. Chop stems fine. Place stems, onions and butter in medium glass mixing bowl.

2 Microwave **3 minutes** on **MED. HIGH (Roast),** or until onions are tender. Stir in sour cream; add cream cheese.

3 Microwave **2½ minutes** on **MED. HIGH (Roast),** or until cream cheese is softened; stir well. Divide mixture in half. Stir ingredients from each variation, below, into each half of the mixture. Fill mushroom caps with the cream cheese mixtures.

4 Microwave **5 to 10 minutes** on **MED. HIGH (Roast),** or until hot.

RECIPE VARIATIONS

MEXICAN MUSHROOMS
Add 2 tablespoons chopped green chilies and ½ cup shredded Monterey Jack cheese to ½ of basic recipe. Garnish each mushroom with one strip of pimento.

ITALIAN MUSHROOMS
Add 6 slices crisp bacon, crumbled, 10 black olives, chopped, ½ teaspoon oregano leaves and ½ teaspoon sweet basil leaves to ½ of basic recipe. Garnish each mushroom with dried parsley flakes.
About 36 Mushrooms

MUNCH MIX

½ cup butter or margarine
1 pkg. (0.6 oz.) Italian salad
   dressing mix
2 cups salted peanuts
1 cup pecan halves
2 cups pretzel sticks
2 cups toasted oat cereal

1 Place butter in 13 x 9-inch glass baking dish.

2 Microwave about **1½ to 2 minutes** on **MED. HIGH (Roast),** or until melted. Stir in seasoning mix and remaining ingredients.

3 Microwave **2 to 4 minutes** on **HIGH,** or until heated through.
About 7 Cups Mix
TIP: Substitute ½ teaspoon garlic salt, ½ teaspoon celery seed and ½ teaspoon Worcestershire sauce for Italian salad dressing mix.

HOT SPICED CIDER

2 quarts apple cider
4 cinnamon sticks
16 whole allspice
16 whole cloves
2 tablespoons packed brown
   sugar
2 lemons, sliced
2 oranges, sliced

1 Combine all ingredients in 3-quart glass bowl.

2 Microwave **14 to 18 minutes,** on **HIGH,** or until hot and bubbly (about 160°F.). Stir; remove spices and serve.
About 8 (8 oz.) Servings
TIP: Make 1 serving. Combine ½ cinnamon stick, 2 whole allspice, 2 whole cloves, ½ teaspoon brown sugar, 1 lemon and 1 orange slice in 8 oz. glass mug. Fill with cider. Microwave **2 to 2½ minutes,** on **HIGH,** or until hot.

Appetizers & Beverages

SPICY FRANKS
1 jar (10 oz.) currant jelly
3 tablespoons prepared mustard
1 lb. skinless franks (about 10)

1 Combine jelly and mustard in 1½-quart glass casserole.

2 Microwave for about **4 to 5 minutes** on **MED. HIGH (Roast),** or until jelly melts. Beat well with rotary beater to blend in mustard.

3 Cut each frank crosswise into 6 pieces. Stir into jelly mixture and continue cooking for **3 to 4 minutes** on **HIGH,** or until franks are hot. Serve in chafing dish with toothpicks.
About 60 Appetizers
TIP: Substitute 2 packages (8 oz. each) cocktail franks for skinless franks.

CRYSTALLIZED ORANGE NUTS
¼ cup orange juice
1 cup sugar
2 cups pecan halves

1 Combine orange juice and sugar in 2-quart (12 x 7) glass baking dish; mix well. Stir in pecans.

2 Microwave for **6 minutes** on **MED. HIGH (Roast).** Stir and continue cooking for **8 to 12 minutes** on **MED. HIGH (Roast),** or until syrup crystalizes. Spread, separate and cool glazed nuts on buttered cookie sheet.
About 3 Cups Nuts

SWEET AND SOUR MEATBALLS
1 lb. ground beef
¼ cup chopped onion
1 egg, beaten
1 teaspoon salt
¼ teaspoon pepper
2 tablespoons water
Sauce
1 tablespoon butter or margarine
1 small onion, chopped
1 cup catsup
1½ tablespoons packed brown sugar
1½ tablespoon lemon juice
1 tablespoon soy sauce

1 Combine all meatball ingredients in medium mixing bowl; mix well. Shape into 20 (1-inch) meatballs. Place in 9-inch round glass baking dish. Cover with wax paper.

2 Microwave for **8 to 9 minutes** on **MED. HIGH (Roast);** drain and rearrange meatballs. Pour Sauce over meatballs and continue cooking for **3 to 5 minutes** on **MED. HIGH (Roast),** or until hot.

Sauce: Place butter and onion in 1-quart glass casserole. Microwave for about **2 to 3 minutes** on **HIGH,** or until onion is partly cooked. Stir in remaining ingredients.
20 Meatballs
RECIPE VARIATION
GLAZED MEATBALLS: Substitute 1 package (¾ oz.) brown gravy mix, ½ cup water, ½ cup apple or currant jelly and 2 tablespoons catsup for all Sauce ingredients. Increase final cooking time by 3 to 4 minutes.

HOT ORIENTAL CHESTNUTS
½ cup soy sauce
½ teaspoon ginger
½ can (8 oz.) water chestnuts, cut into halves
6 slices bacon, cut into thirds
Sugar

1 Combine all ingredients, except bacon and sugar, in 2-cup glass measure. Marinate for 3 to 4 hours.

2 Roll water chestnuts in bacon pieces; coat with sugar and skewer with toothpick. Place on microwave roasting rack in 2-quart (12 x 7) glass baking dish.

3 Microwave for **7 to 10 minutes** on **HIGH,** or until bacon is crisp.
18 Appetizers

TOMATO SIPPER

1 can (18 oz.) tomato juice
1 can (10½ oz.) condensed beef broth
¼ cup lemon juice
1 teaspoon horseradish
1 teaspoon dried parsley flakes
½ teaspoon celery salt
2 to 4 tablespoons dry sherry or Madeira

1 Combine all ingredients, except sherry, in 4-cup glass measure.

2 Microwave for **8 to 9 minutes** on **HIGH,** or until hot (about 160° F.). Pour into six (6 oz.) cups or mugs. Stir 1 to 2 teaspoons sherry into each cup. **About 6 (6 oz.) Servings.**

FRENCH HOT CHOCOLATE

½ cup water
3 squares (1 oz. each) unsweetened chocolate
½ cup sugar
Dash salt
½ cup whipping cream, whipped
Milk

1 Place water and chocolate in 2-cup glass measure.

2 Microwave for about **2 minutes** on **HIGH,** or until melted. Blend in sugar and salt.

3 Microwave for about **1 minute** on **HIGH,** or until hot. Cool. Fold in whipped cream. Refrigerate until served.

4 To make 1 serving, combine 3 tablespoons chocolate mixture and desired amount of milk in individual (6 oz.) glass cups or mugs.

5 Microwave for **1½ to 2 minutes** on **HIGH,** or until hot (about 160° F.). About 1 Cup Chocolate Mixture Makes About 5 (6 oz.) Servings.
TIP: Add a marshmallow during the last 10 to 15 seconds of heating.
RECIPE VARIATIONS
MINTED CHOCOLATE DRINK: Add ⅛ teaspoon peppermint extract to milk. Garnish with peppermint stick.
MOCHA CHOCOLATE DRINK: Add 1 to 2 tablespoons coffee liqueur to milk.

IRISH COFFEE

3½ cups water
2 tablespoons instant coffee
2 tablespoons sugar
⅓ to ½ cup Irish whiskey
¼ cup whipping cream, whipped

1 Combine all ingredients, except whiskey and whipping cream, in 4-cup glass measure.

2 Microwave for **8 to 10 minutes** on **HIGH,** or until hot (about 200° F.). Stir in whiskey. Pour into mugs or glasses. Top with dollop of whipped cream.
About 6 (6 oz.) Servings
RECIPE VARIATIONS
SPANISH COFFEE: Add 1 teaspoon grated orange rind with sugar. Substitute ⅓ to ½ cup orange-flavored liqueur for whiskey.
VIENNESE COFFEE: Decrease sugar to 1½ tablespoons; add 2 cinnamon sticks and 8 whole cloves with sugar. Microwave as directed in basic recipe; omit whiskey.
FRENCH COFFEE: Decrease water to 2 cups. Add ½ teaspoon peppermint extract with water; omit sugar. Reduce cooking time 2 to 3 minutes. Substitute 1 cup whipping cream for whiskey. Microwave for an additional **1 to 1½ minutes** on **MED. HIGH (Roast),** or until warm (about 150° F.). Omit dollops of whipped cream.

Breads

Quick breads microwave without the brown crust we've come to expect. But top with spices, brown sugar, cornmeal and/or frosting for appearance and even better taste. Yeast breads microwave with an even texture, tender edges and no brown crust. (A disadvantage to some; an advantage to others.) Quick breads start baking on **MEDIUM (Simmer)** and finish on **HIGH** to set the batter. Yeast breads are microwaved on **MEDIUM (Simmer).** As you try these and other bread recipes, remember to follow instructions carefully for best results.

QUICK COFFEE CAKE

2 cups biscuit mix
2 tablespoons sugar
1 carton (8 oz.) sour cream
1 egg
1 tablespoon sugar
½ teaspoon cinnamon

Filling

¼ cup biscuit mix
¼ cup packed brown sugar
2 tablespoons butter or margarine
¼ cup chopped nuts

1 Combine all coffee cake ingredients, except 1 tablespoon sugar and cinnamon, in medium mixing bowl; mix well. Divide dough in half; spread half in 9-inch round glass baking dish. Sprinkle Filling over top. Drop remaining dough by teaspoonfuls over Filling (filling will show through). Combine 1 tablespoon sugar and cinnamon; sprinkle over top.

2 Microwave **10 minutes** on **MEDIUM (Simmer).**

3 Microwave 4 to 6 minutes on **HIGH,** or until toothpick inserted near center comes out clean. Let stand 2 minutes.

4 Filling: Combine biscuit mix and brown sugar in small mixing bowl; cut in butter. Stir in nuts.

About 6 Servings
RECIPE VARIATION
APPLE COFFEE CAKE:
Substitute 1 carton (8 oz.) spicy apple yogurt for sour cream.

BRAN MUFFINS

1 cup water
3 cups all bran cereal
½ cup butter or margarine
1½ cups sugar
2 eggs
2½ cups unsifted all-purpose flour
2 teaspoons soda
2 cups buttermilk or sour milk

1 Microwave water to boiling in 1-cup glass measure, about **2 minutes** on **HIGH.**

2 Place bran cereal in large mixing bowl. Stir in water until moistened. Add butter and let mixture stand until softened. Stir in sugar and eggs; beat well. Blend in flour, soda, and buttermilk. Mix well. Spoon batter into paper-lined custard cups, filling half-full. Store remaining batter in refrigerator for up to 6 weeks.

3 Microwave following cooking times and settings below:
2 muffins—**MEDIUM (Simmer) 1 minute; High 30 seconds.**
4 muffins—**MEDIUM (Simmer) 2 minutes; HIGH 1 to 1½ minutes.**
6 muffins—**MEDIUM (Simmer) 4½ minutes; HIGH 1½ to 2 minutes.**
TIP: Remove from custard cups immediately to prevent muffins from becomin soggy.
40 to 48 Muffins.

HOW TO BAKE FROZEN BREAD DOUGH

1 Grease one 1 lb. loaf frozen bread dough; place in greased 9 x 5-inch glass loaf dish. Cover loosely with wax paper. Place dish of dough in 12 x 7-inch glass baking dish. Pour 2 cups hot water (about 130°F.) into baking dish.

2 Microwave **15 minutes** on **WARM.**

3 Let stand in oven 10 minutes. Repeat these two steps until dough is just above top of dish, about 4 to 5 times. Remove dish of water and uncover bread.

4 Microwave 10 to 12 minutes on **MEDIUM (Simmer),** or until no longer doughy.
1 Loaf Bread
TIP: Frozen bread dough must be fresh or it will not raise fully.
For browned crust bake conventionally after proofing.

Cakes

Here are some tips to help you in microwaving cakes. Prepare batter as directed in recipe or on cake mix package. Use glass dish specified in chart below. (Not always the same as suggested on the recipe or package.) Do not fill dish more than half full. Instead, use extra batter to make cupcakes, as directed in the chart. Line the bottom of flat dishes with wax paper if cake is to be unmolded. When cake is cooked in a large bowl, press a glass into the center of the batter, open end up. Or, use a ceramic or plastic bundt-type dish. Start microwaving on **MEDIUM (Simmer)** to raise batter; finish on **HIGH** to set the cake. The cake is done when a toothpick inserted near center comes out clean. Let cake stand 5 minutes to set. Turn out on serving plate to cool or cool in dish on wire rack.

Cake Mix	Glass Utensil	First Setting and Time	Second Setting and Time
1 pkg. (9 oz.) 1 layer	9-inch round dish	**MEDIUM (Simmer)** 8 min.	**HIGH** 2 to 4 min.
1 pkg. (17 to 18½ oz.) 1 cake	12 x 7-inch baking dish	**MEDIUM (Simmer)** 11 min.	**HIGH** 3 to 6 min.
		MEDIUM (Simmer)	**HIGH**
2 cupcakes	Paper cupcake liners in individual custard cups	1 min.	15 to 30 sec.
4 cupcakes		3 min.	30 to 45 sec.
6 cupcakes		4 min.	1 to 1½ min.
8 cupcakes		5 min.	1½ to 2 min.

FIVE-MINUTE SNOWY WHITE FROSTING

1 cup sugar
½ cup water
¼ teaspoon cream of tartar
Dash salt
2 egg whites
1 teaspoon vanilla

1 Combine sugar, water, cream of tartar and salt in 2-cup glass measure.

2 Microwave **4 to 5 minutes** on **MED. HIGH (Roast),** or until mixture boils (about 200°F.).

3 Beat 2 egg whites in small mixer bowl until soft peaks form. Gradually pour in hot syrup; beat about 5 minutes or until thick and fluffy. Blend in vanilla.

Frosts 12 x 7-inch or Two 9-inch Layers

Pictured: Cake made from a mix, chart above.
Five-Minute Snowy White Frosting, recipe above.

Candy

Candy is dandy in your microwave oven. Remember to microwave on **MED. HIGH (Roast)** so sugar syrup boils, sugar dissolves and syrup blends into candy. Use containers 2 to 3 times larger than quantity to prevent boil-overs and cover candy and snacks when specified. Use a glass plate or stretch plastic wrap tightly across bowl. Pierce wrap so steam escapes during cooking. Stir candy during cooking so heat is equalized and candy cooks smooth. WATCH CANDY CLOSELY because a microwave oven cooks fast. Check with a candy thermometer. (Remove candy from oven first unless using a microwave candy thermometer.)

FUDGE

3 cups sugar
¾ cup butter or margarine
1 can (5 oz.) evaporated milk
1 pkg. (12 oz.) semi-sweet chocolate pieces
1 jar (10 oz.) marshmallow creme
1 cup chopped nuts
1 teaspoon vanilla

1 Combine sugar, butter and milk in buttered large glass mixing bowl. Cover with plastic wrap.

2 Microwave **10 minutes** on **MED. HIGH (Roast).** Stir and continue cooking on **MED. HIGH (Roast)** for **5 to 8 minutes** or until mixture forms a soft ball in cold water. Stir in chocolate pieces until melted. Fold in marshmallow creme, nuts and vanilla.

3 Pour into buttered 13 x 9-inch pan. Chill until firm; cut into squares.

74 Fudge Squares

DIVINITY

2 cups granulated sugar
½ cup cold water
1 teaspoon vinegar
1 egg white
½ teaspoon vanilla
½ cup chopped nuts

1 Combine sugar, water and vinegar in a buttered 4-cup glass measure; cover with plastic wrap.

2 Microwave **12 to 17 minutes** on **MED. HIGH (Roast)** or until candy forms a firm ball in cold water (240°F.). Meanwhile, beat egg white in medium mixer bowl until stiff peaks form. Pour candy syrup in thin stream into egg white, beating constantly with mixer. Add vanilla; beat until mixture is stiff. Fold in nuts. Drop mixture by teaspoonfuls onto wax paper; cool.

Approximately 30 Candy Pieces
TIP: For extra color, add ¼ cup chopped candied cherries when adding nuts.

CARAMELS

1 cup butter or margarine
2¼ cups brown sugar
1 cup light corn syrup
1 can (15 oz.) sweetened condensed milk
Dash salt
1 teaspoon vanilla

1 Place butter in large buttered mixing bowl. Microwave **1 to 2 minutes** on **MED. HIGH (Roast)** to melt. Blend in brown sugar, syrup, condensed milk and salt. Cover with plastic wrap.

2 Microwave **10 to 12 minutes** on **HIGH;** stir well. Microwave, uncovered, **16 to 20 minutes** on **MED. HIGH (Roast)** (240°F.) or until candy forms ball in cold water. Mix in vanilla and pour into greased 12 x 7-inch baking dish. Cool to room temperature before cutting. Cut and wrap in individual pieces.
About 84 One-inch Candies

Desserts

Enjoy tender, juicy fruit desserts. Fresh fruits microwave quickly on **HIGH**—holding shape and retaining full flavor. Canned fruits are already cooked. Use **REHEAT** to prevent mushing. Fruit is cooked when it's soft and tender.

FRESH CHERRIES JUBILEE

2 teaspoons cornstarch
¼ cup water
½ cup red currant jelly
2 cups fresh sweet cherries,
    washed and pitted
¼ cup brandy
Vanilla ice cream

1 Combine cornstarch and water in 1-quart glass casserole until smooth; stir in jelly and cherries.

2 Microwave for **6 to 9 minutes** on **HIGH,** or until hot (about 200° F.).

3 Measure brandy into 1-cup glass measure.

4 Microwave for **15 to 30 seconds** on **HIGH,** or until warm. Pour brandy over cherry sauce and ignite. Immediately spoon sauce over ice cream.
About 2 Cups Sauce

RECIPE VARIATIONS

CHERRIES JUBILEE: Omit cornstarch and water in basic recipe. Reduce red currant jelly to ¼ cup; add ½ teaspoon grated orange rind. Substitute 1 can (21 oz.) cherry pie filling for fresh cherries.
APRICOT JUBILEE: Increase cornstarch to 1 tablespoon in basic recipe. Substitute apple jelly for red currant jelly and 1 can (16 oz.) apricot halves, drained, for fresh cherries. Reduce cooking time to **1 to 2 minutes.**

CRUNCHY APPLE CRISP

6 cups peeled, cored and sliced
    cooking apples
⅔ cup quick-cooking rolled oats
⅓ cup unsifted all-purpose flour
¾ cup packed brown sugar
½ teaspoon nutmeg
½ teaspoon cinnamon
¼ cup butter or margarine

1 Place apple slices in 2-quart (8 x 8) glass baking dish. Combine remaining ingredients, except butter, in medium mixing bowl. Cut in butter until crumbly. Sprinkle over apples.

2 Microwave for **12 to 16 minutes** on **HIGH** or until apples are tender.
About 6 Servings

RECIPE VARIATIONS

CHERRY CRISP: Substitute 1 can (21-oz) cherry pie filling for apples.
RHUBARB CRISP: Substitute 3 cups diced, fresh or frozen rhubarb and ⅓ cup sugar for apples.
AMBROSIA CRISP: Substitute 6 medium oranges, peeled and sectioned. 3 medium bananas, sliced, ¾ cup flaked coconut. 2 tablespoons lemon juice, and 2 tablespoons all-purpose flour for apples.
PEACH CRISP: Substitute 1 can (21-oz) peach pie filling for apples. Combine 2 tablespoons sugar and ½ teaspoon cinnamon; stir into peach pie filling. Sprinkle topping over fruit as directed in basic recipe.

HOT PINK PEARS

6 ripe winter pears
6 whole cloves
1 cup sugar
½ cup sweet vermouth
¼ cup water
½ teaspoon red food coloring
Whipped cream if desired

1 Peel pears; leave stem. Stick 1 whole clove into each pear. Combine remaining ingredients, except whipped cream, in 1½-quart glass casserole. Add pears; cover with glass lid.

2 Microwave for **6 minutes** on **HIGH.** Baste pears; turn over, and recover. Continue cooking for **6 to 9 minutes** on **HIGH,** or until tender. Serve in individual bowls; garnish with whipped cream.
6 Servings

Eggs & Cheese

First a Don't: Don't microwave eggs in the shell because they may explode even at low settings. And don't reheat whole, hardcooked eggs in a microwave oven because they, too, may explode. But most everything else is possible if you remember that gentle heat is the secret to tender-light egg and cheese dishes. Cheese dishes are smooth, cream cheeses and spreads melt beautifully on **MED. HIGH (Roast)** which prevents separation and curdling. Coverings are important in these recipes, too, so follow instructions carefully.

BASIC OMELET

2 eggs
½ teaspoon dry parsley, optional
¼ teaspoon salt
Dash pepper
1 tablespoon water
1½ teaspoons butter or margarine
¼ cup shredded Cheddar cheese

1 In a 2-cup measure beat well, the eggs, parsley, salt and pepper.

2 Preheat the browning grill according to manufacturer's instructions on **HIGH.** Spread butter on preheated browning grill and pour on egg mixture. Microwave **1½ to 2 minutes** on **MED. HIGH (Roast).** Top with cheese, fold omelet and let stand 30 to 40 seconds or until cheese is melted.
1 Serving

QUICHE LORRAINE

½ lb. bacon (about 8 slices)
1 (9-inch) baked pastry shell in glass pie plate
1 can (4 oz.) mushroom stems and pieces, drained
1½ cups shredded Cheddar cheese
3 green onions, sliced
1¼ cups light cream
3 eggs
½ teaspoon salt
⅛ teaspoon pepper

1 Arrange bacon in single layer in 13 x 9-inch glass baking dish.

2 Microwave **6 to 9 minutes** on **HIGH,** or until crisp; cool. Crumble into bottom of baked crust. Sprinkle mushrooms, cheese and onions on top.

3 Measure cream in 4-cup glass measure and microwave **2 to 3½ minutes** on **HIGH,** or until hot but not boiling. Beat in remaining ingredients; pour over bacon-cheese mixture.

4 Microwave **20 to 27 minutes** on **MEDIUM (Simmer),** or until almost set in center. Let stand 5 minutes before serving.
5 to 6 Servings

POACHED EGGS

1 cup water
¼ teaspoon vinegar
4 eggs

1 Place water and vinegar in 1-quart glass casserole.

2 Microwave **2½ to 4½ minutes** on **HIGH,** until boiling. Break eggs carefully into hot water. Cover tightly with glass lid or wax paper.

3 Microwave **2 to 3 minutes** on **MED. HIGH (Roast).** Let stand, covered, 1 minute before serving.
TIP: For 1 poached egg, place ¼ cup water and ¼ teaspoon vinegar in individual 6 oz. custard cup. Microwave **1½ to 2½ minutes** on **HIGH,** or until boiling. Break egg into hot water and cover tightly with wax paper. Microwave **30 to 60 seconds** on **MED. HIGH (Roast).** For 2 poached eggs, place ½ cup water and ¼ teaspoon vinegar in 2 individual 6 oz. custard cups. Microwave **2 to 2½ minutes** on **HIGH,** or until boiling. Break eggs into hot water and cover tightly with wax paper. Microwave **45 seconds to 1 minute** on **MED. HIGH (Roast).**
4 Poached Eggs

Bacon and Scrambled Eggs

Place 8 slices of bacon on microwave roasting rack in 13 x 9-inch baking dish. Place dish on rack in lower rack position.

Prepare Scrambled Egg Mixture using 6 eggs, recipe is on page 44. Cover with glass lid or wax paper. Place on floor of oven.

Microwave **8 minutes** on **HIGH.** Stir eggs; recover. Microwave **4 to 7 minutes** on **HIGH** or until eggs are firm but still moist. Let stand 3 to 5 minutes before serving. If crisper bacon is desired continue cooking bacon, alone, for **1 to 2 minutes** on **HIGH.**

TIP: Sweet Rolls can be warmed with this meal by placing them next to the eggs during the last 1 to 2 minutes of cooking.

SEAFOOD SCRAMBLED EGGS

8 eggs
1 can (10¾ oz.) condensed cream of shrimp soup
¼ teaspoon salt
⅛ teaspoon hot pepper sauce
1 can (4 oz.) mushroom stems and pieces, drained
2 green onions, finely sliced

1 Combine eggs, soup and seasonings in 1½-quart glass casserole; beat well. Stir in remaining ingredients. Cover with glass lid.

2 Microwave for **7 minutes** on **MED. HIGH (Roast).** Stir; recover, and continue cooking for about **5 to 7 minutes** on **MED. HIGH (Roast),** or until mixture is liquid only in the center. Stir gently with fork to scramble and cook excess liquid. Let stand, covered, 3 minutes before serving.

6 to 8 Servings
RECIPE VARIATION
ZUCCHINI SCRAMBLED EGGS: Substitute 1 can (10¾ oz.) condensed cream of mushroom soup for cream of shrimp soup, and ½ teaspoon oregano leaves for hot pepper sauce. Substitute 1 small zucchini, quartered and sliced, and ⅓ cup grated Parmesan cheese for mushrooms and green onion.

SAUSAGE EGG NESTS

1 package (12 oz.) bulk pork sausage
1 cup shredded Swiss cheese
1 tablespoon dried parsley flakes
4 eggs
Salt
Pepper
½ cup light cream

1 Crumble sausage into 2-quart (8 x 8) glass baking dish. Cover with wax paper.

2 Microwave for **5 to 6 minutes** on **HIGH,** or until browned. Drain well. Stir in ¾ cup of the cheese and parsley. Spread over bottom of dish, making small indentations or nests. Break eggs into indentations. Sprinkle with salt and pepper. Pour cream over top; sprinkle with remaining ¼ cup shredded cheese. Cover with wax paper.

3 Microwave for **8 to 12 minutes** on **MED. HIGH (Roast),** or until eggs are cooked to desired doneness. Let stand, covered, 2 minutes before serving.

About 4 Servings

CHEESY GRITS

3 cups water
1 teaspoon salt
¾ cup quick-cooking grits
2 eggs, slightly beaten
2 cups shredded Cheddar cheese
1 tablespoon butter or margarine
¼ teaspoon salt
Dash cayenne pepper

1 Combine water and salt in 2-quart glass casserole. Cover with glass lid.

2 Microwave for **6 to 9 minutes** on **HIGH** or until boiling. Stir in grits; recover.

3 Microwave for **3 to 4 minutes** on **MED. HIGH (Roast),** or until thickened. Let stand, covered, 3 minutes to set. Stir in remaining ingredients. Do not cover.

4 Microwave for **22 to 24 minutes** on **MEDIUM (Simmer),** or until almost set in center. Let stand 5 minutes before serving.

About 6 Servings

Fish & Seafood

Soon you'll be fixing your catch to moist, flaky, delicate perfection in minutes. Remember to thaw frozen fish or seafood before cooking and to arrange pieces in the glass baking dish with thicker edges and larger pieces toward the outside, smaller pieces and tail ends toward the center of the dish. (When cooking lobster tails, split each tail through top or bottom shell to prevent curling during cooking.) Cover with glass lid or wax paper tucked tightly across the top. Fish is done if it flakes when lifted gently with a fork near the center. Let stand, covered, for 5 minutes to complete cooking.

Fish/Seafood	Weight	Glass Utensil	Minutes on HIGH	Internal Temperature
FILLETS: Sole, Halibut, Perch, Pike, Whitefish, Flounder, Snapper	1 lb.	12 x 7-inch baking dish	**6 to 7**	140°F.
	2 lb.		**9 to 12**	140°F.
WHOLE FISH	1½ to 1¾ lb.	13 x 9-inch baking dish	**10 to 14**	140°F.
SHRIMP OR BAY SCALLOPS	½ lb.	1-quart casserole	**4 to 5**	—
SALMON STEAKS (4)	¾ inch thick (each)	12 x 7-inch baking dish	**10 to 12**	140°F.
LOBSTER TAILS (2)	½ to ¾ lb. each	12 x 7-inch baking dish	**10 to 12**	—

LEMON DILL SAUCE

3 tablespoons all-purpose flour
½ cup light cream
½ teaspoon salt
1 teaspoon dill weed
1 tablespoon lemon juice
1 cup fish poaching liquid
3 tablespoons butter or margarine

1 Combine all ingredients, except poaching liquid and butter in small mixing bowl; beat with rotary beater until smooth.

2 Beat in reserved poaching liquid and add butter or margarine. Microwave about **5 minutes on MED. HIGH (Roast),** or until mixture thickens (about 175°F.). Beat lightly. Serve over fish.
About 4 Servings

CUCUMBER SAUCE

1 can (10¾ oz.) condensed cream of shrimp soup
½ cup sour cream
½ cup finely chopped cucumber
2 green onions, sliced
½ teaspoon salt
⅛ teaspoon pepper

1 Combine all sauce ingredients in small glass mixing bowl. Microwave **4 minutes** on **MED. HIGH (Roast).** Stir and continue microwaving **2 to 4 minutes** on **MED. HIGH (Roast).**

2 Stir sauce and let stand 3 minutes before serving. Pour sauce over fish.
6 to 8 Servings

PIQUANT SAUCE

¼ cup butter or margarine
½ teaspoon dry mustard
1½ teaspoons dried parsley flakes
⅛ teaspoon garlic powder
1½ teaspoons lemon juice

1 Place butter in 1-cup glass measure.

2 Microwave on **MED. HIGH (Roast)** for about **1½ minutes** or until melted. Add mustard, parsley flakes, garlic powder and lemon juice. Pour sauce over fish to serve.
4 Servings

Pictured: Salmon Steak, chart above, with Lemon Dill Sauce, recipe above.

TURBAN OF FLOUNDER

2 tablespoons butter or margarine
2 tablespoons finely chopped
   onion
1 can (4 oz.) mushroom stems
   and pieces, drained
1 cup herb-seasoned stuffing mix
¼ cup grated Parmesan cheese
1 jar (2 oz.) chopped pimento
½ teaspoon celery salt
¼ teaspoon pepper
1 lb. frozen flounder fillets, thawed
1 cup Bechamel Sauce, page 113

1 Place butter, onion and mushrooms in 1½-quart glass casserole.

2 Microwave about **3 to 4 minutes** on **MED. HIGH (Roast),** or until onion is partly cooked. Stir in remaining ingredients, except fish and Bechamel Sauce; set aside. Lightly butter four 6 oz. custard cups. Coil one fillet around inside of each cup or cut fish to line inside of cup. Evenly divide stuffing among the 4 custard cups. Cover with wax paper.

3 Microwave **8 to 10 minutes** on **MED. HIGH (Roast),** or until fish flakes easily (about 140° F.). Let stand, covered, 5 minutes before serving. Invert on serving platter. Serve with hot Bechamel Sauce.
About 4 Servings

Fish & Seafood

WINE SCAMPI

2 tablespoons butter or margarine
1 clove garlic, finely chopped
3 tablespoons dry white wine
1 lb. raw fresh shrimp or scampi
Parsley, if desired

1 Place butter, garlic and wine in 1½-quart glass casserole.

2 Microwave for **2 minutes** on **HIGH.** Stir in shrimp and continue cooking for about **4 to 5 minutes** on **HIGH,** or until shrimp turns pink. Let stand 5 minutes before serving. Garnish with snipped parsley.
2 to 3 Servings

SALMON-RICE LOAF

1 tablespoon butter or margarine
¼ cup chopped onion
⅓ cup chopped celery
1 can (16 oz.) salmon, drained and flaked
1 cup cooked rice, page 99
2 eggs, beaten
1 teaspoon dried parsley flakes
½ teaspoon salt
¼ teaspoon pepper
1 teaspoon lemon juice

1 Place butter, onion and celery in medium glass mixing bowl.

2 Microwave for **2 to 3 minutes** on **HIGH,** or until vegetables are partly cooked. Add remaining ingredients; mix well. Pat into 9 x 5 glass loaf dish. Cover with wax paper.

3 Microwave for **10 to 14 minutes** on **MED. HIGH (Roast),** or until hot in center (about 160° F.). Let stand, covered, 5 minutes before serving.
About 4 Servings

HERB FILLETS

2 tablespoons butter or margarine
1 clove garlic, finely chopped
¼ cup finely chopped onion
1 tablespoon lemon juice
2 teaspoons dried parsley flakes
½ teaspoon salt
¼ teaspoon tarragon leaves
⅛ teaspoon chervil leaves or thyme leaves
1 lb. frozen fish fillets, thawed
¼ cup dry bread crumbs

1 Place butter, garlic and onion in small glass mixing bowl.

2 Microwave for **1 to 2 minutes** on **HIGH,** or until onion is partly cooked. Stir in remaining ingredients, except fish and bread crumbs.

3 Arrange fillets in 2-quart (12 x 7) glass baking dish with thick edges toward outside of dish. Spoon about ½ of butter mixture over fillets. Stir bread crumbs into remaining butter mixture; sprinkle on top of fillets.

4 Microwave for **7 to 8 minutes** on **HIGH,** or until fish flakes easily (about 140° F.). Let stand 5 minutes before serving.
About 4 Servings

SAUCY FISH STICKS

2 packages (8 oz. each) frozen fish sticks
Tomato-Bacon Sauce
3 slices bacon
1 can (10¾ oz.) condensed tomato soup
2 tablespoons water
¼ cup chopped celery
2 tablespoons chopped onion
¼ teaspoon ground oregano
⅛ teaspoon garlic powder

1 Arrange frozen fish sticks in 3-quart (13 x 9) glass baking dish; set aside.

2 Arrange bacon in single layer in 1½-quart glass casserole.

3 Microwave for **3 to 3½ minutes** on **HIGH,** or until bacon is crisp; drain. Crumble bacon. Stir in remaining Tomato-Bacon Sauce ingredients; cover.

4 Place fish on upper rack position of oven and sauce on floor of oven.

5 Microwave both for **10 to 14 minutes** on **HIGH,** or until fish and sauce are hot (about 160° F.). Stir sauce and let stand 5 minutes before serving. Serve sauce over fish.
About 4 Servings.

Salmon-Rice Loaf, Broccoli Spears, and Lemon Sauce

Prepare Salmon-Rice Loaf recipe page 84, through step 2. Place salmon loaf on rack in lower rack position. Place 1 package (10 oz.) frozen Broccoli Spears in a flat dish, slit pouch. Place dish on rack with Salmon Loaf. Prepare Lemon Sauce, recipe page 114, through step 1. Place Lemon Sauce under Salmon Loaf on floor of oven. Microwave **14 minutes** on **HIGH**; stir sauce. Microwave **6 to 10 minutes** on **HIGH** or until broccoli is hot and sauce thick.

CREAMED TUNA

2 tablespoons butter or margarine
¼ cup chopped onion
2 tablespoons chopped green pepper
1 can (6½ oz.) tuna, drained, rinsed and flaked
¼ cup unsifted all-purpose flour
1½ cups milk
¼ teaspoon salt
⅛ teaspoon pepper

1 Place butter, onion, green pepper and tuna in 4-cup glass measure.

2 Microwave for **3 to 4 minutes** on **HIGH.** Combine remaining ingredients in small bowl until smooth; stir into tuna-vegetable mixture. Continue cooking for **4 to 9 minutes** on **HIGH,** or until thickened (about 160°F.). Let stand 5 minutes before serving.
About 4 Servings
RECIPE VARIATIONS
CREAMED SALMON: Substitute 1 can (6½ oz.) salmon, drained and flaked, for tuna in basic recipe.
EASY CREAMED TUNA: Reduce butter to 1 tablespoon in basic recipe. Substitute 1 can (10¾ oz.) condensed cream of mushroom soup and ¼ cup milk for flour and milk. Stir soup and seasonings into cooked tuna vegetable mixture in Step 2. Microwave for **5 to 8 minutes** on **MED. HIGH (Roast),** or until thickened (about 160°F.). Let stand 5 minutes before serving.

SHRIMP JAMBALAYA

2 tablespoons butter or margarine
½ cup chopped onion
½ cup chopped celery
¼ cup chopped green pepper
1 lb. frozen cooked shrimp, thawed
2 cups cubed cooked ham
1 cup quick-cooking rice
2 teaspoons dried parsley flakes
½ teaspoon salt
¼ teaspoon garlic powder
¼ teaspoon thyme leaves
⅛ teaspoon ground cloves
⅛ teaspoon cayenne pepper
1 can (16 oz.) whole tomatoes
½ cup water

1 Place butter, onion, celery and green pepper in 2½-quart glass casserole.

2 Microwave for **4 to 5 minutes** on **HIGH,** or until vegetables are partly cooked. Stir in remaining ingredients; cover with glass lid.

3 Microwave for **7 minutes** on **HIGH.** Stir and continue cooking for **7 to 10 minutes** on **HIGH,** or until heated through (about 150°F.). Let stand, covered, 5 minutes before serving.
4 to 6 Servings

WILD FISH BAKE

2 packages (11 oz. each) frozen white and wild rice mix
1 lb. frozen fish fillets, thawed
½ cup mayonnaise or salad dressing
½ cup sour cream
2 tablespoons prepared mustard
½ teaspoon salt
½ teaspoon dill weed

1 Place rice pouches in 2-quart (12 x 7) glass baking dish; slit pouches.

2 Microwave for about **5 to 7 minutes** on **HIGH,** or until thawed. Empty pouches into dish; spread over bottom of dish. Arrange fillets over rice with thick edges toward outside of dish. Cover with wax paper.

3 Microwave for **7 minutes** on **HIGH.** Combine remaining ingredients in small bowl; pour over fish; recover.

4 Microwave for **4 to 7 minutes** on **MED. HIGH (Roast),** or until fish flakes easily (about 140°F.). Let stand, covered, 5 minutes before serving.
About 4 Servings

Main Dishes & Stews

Meat plus vegetables (and sometimes rice or pasta) combine into main dishes and stews that microwave fast in a single glass dish—lets you serve all the nutritious juice along with the meat and vegetables. Main dishes may be mixed ahead of cooking, then refrigerated. Add 5 to 10 minutes to final cooking period when main dish or stew is microwaved directly from the refrigerator.

COQ AU VIN

5 slices bacon
1 can (10¾ oz.) condensed cream of onion soup
½ cup dry red wine or water
3 green onions, sliced
1 clove garlic, finely chopped
1½ teaspoons instant chicken bouillon
1 teaspoon salt
1 teaspoon dried parsley flakes
¼ teaspoon thyme leaves
Dash pepper
2½ to 3 lb. frying chicken, cut into pieces
6 small new red potatoes, peeled and cut in half
2 medium carrots, peeled and sliced
8 ozs. fresh mushrooms, washed

1 Arrange bacon in single layer in 10-inch glass ceramic skillet.

2 Microwave for about **4½ to 6½ minutes** on **HIGH,** or until crisp. Remove bacon; set aside. Drain off fat. Combine soup, wine, onions, garlic, bouillon and seasonings in glass ceramic skillet. Add remaining ingredients, except mushrooms. Cover with glass lid.

3 Microwave for **30 minutes** on **HIGH.** Add mushrooms, crumble bacon over top, and recover.

4 Microwave for **10 to 12 minutes** on **MED. HIGH (Roast),** or until meat cut near bone is no longer pink. Let stand, covered, 5 minutes before serving.
About 6 Servings

BEEF SHORT RIBS AND PARSLEY DUMPLINGS

2 to 2½ lbs. beef short ribs
1 cup catsup
½ cup water
1 tablespoon sugar
1 tablespoon prepared horseradish
1 tablespoon prepared mustard
1 tablespoon vinegar
1 teaspoon salt
⅛ teaspoon pepper
⅛ teaspoon hot pepper sauce
Parsley Dumplings
1 cup biscuit mix
1 tablespoon dried parsley flakes
⅓ cup milk

1 Place ribs, fat-side-down in 10-inch glass ceramic skillet; set aside. Combine remaining ingredients, except dumpling ingredients, in 2-cup glass measure; pour over ribs. Cover with glass lid.

2 Microwave for **10 to 15 minutes** on **HIGH,** or until sauce is hot. Turn ribs over; recover.

3 Microwave for **30 minutes** on **MEDIUM (Simmer).** Drop Parsley Dumplings by tablespoonfuls into hot liquid; recover, and continue cooking for **10 to 12 minutes** on **MEDIUM (Simmer),** or until dumplings are no longer doughy.

Parsley Dumplings: Combine biscuit mix and parsley flakes in medium mixing bowl; stir in milk.
4 to 6 Servings

PORK 'N BEANS

1 lb. lean fresh pork, cut into 1-inch cubes
1 medium onion, chopped
1 can (31 oz.) pork and beans
¼ cup dark molasses
2 tablespoons packed brown sugar
1 tablespoon prepared mustard
2 teaspoons dried parsley flakes
2 teaspoons Worcestershire sauce

1 Place pork and onion in 1½ quart glass casserole. Cover with glass lid.

2 Microwave for **15 to 20 minutes** on **MED. HIGH (Roast),** or until meat is browned; drain. Stir in remaining ingredients. Recover and continue cooking for **10 to 15 minutes,** on **MED. HIGH (Roast),** or until hot (about 150°F.). Let stand, covered, 5 minutes before serving.
About 4 Servings.

GRANDMA'S BEEF STEW

1 to 1¼ lb. beef stew meat
1 lb. red potatoes, cubed
2 carrots, sliced
1 large onion, chopped
2 stalks celery, chopped
1 can (16 oz.) whole kernel corn,
　well drained
1 can (6 oz.) tomato paste
1 cup water
1 tablespoon instant beef bouillon
1 teaspoon salt
¼ teaspoon pepper

1 Combine all ingredients in water-soaked clay pot. Cover with water-soaked lid.

2 Microwave **15 minutes** on **HIGH.** Stir well and recover.

3 Microwave **55 to 60 minutes** on **MEDIUM (Simmer),** or until meat is fork tender. Let stand, covered, 5 minutes before serving.
4 to 6 Servings

SWISS STEAK

3 tablespoons all-purpose flour
1 teaspoon salt
¼ teaspoon pepper
2 lb. beef round steak, cut into
　serving pieces
1 medium onion, chopped
¼ green pepper, chopped
1 can (8 oz.) whole tomatoes
1 can (6 oz.) tomato paste

1 Combine flour and seasonings in shallow dish. Coat meat in seasoned flour; pound into meat. Place meat in water-soaked clay pot. Place onion and green pepper over meat. Add tomatoes and tomato paste. Cover with water-soaked lid.

2 Microwave **10 minutes** on **HIGH.** Rearrange meat pieces; recover.

3 Microwave **55 to 60 minutes** on **MEDIUM (Simmer),** or until meat is fork tender. Let stand, covered, 5 minutes before serving.
4 to 6 Servings

CHILI

1 lb. ground beef
1 medium onion, chopped
½ cup chopped green pepper
1 can (6 oz.) tomato paste
1 can (16 oz.) whole tomatoes
1 can (15½ oz.) kidney beans,
　undrained
½ cup water
1 teaspoon salt
¼ teaspoon garlic powder
2 to 3 teaspoons chili powder

1 Crumble ground beef in 2-quart glass casserole. Stir in onion and green pepper. Cover with glass lid.

2 Microwave about **5 to 6 minutes** on **HIGH,** or until meat is browned. Drain and stir in remaining ingredients; recover.

3 Microwave **14 to 18 minutes** on **MED. HIGH (Roast),** or until hot (about 150°F.). Let stand, covered, 5 minutes before serving.
4 to 6 Servings
TIP: Sprinkle shredded Cheddar cheese over bowls of chili, if desired.

MAKE-A-MEAL
Add Garlic Bread

French bread dipped in Sliced Cheesy Garlic Butter, recipe page 114, can be warmed with the Lasagna. Cook the Lasagna on the rack in the lower rack position according to the directions above. Place the garlic bread, wrapped in paper towel, on the floor of the oven during the last 2 to 3 minutes of cooking.

LASAGNA

1 pkg. (12 oz.) bulk pork sausage
1 lb. ground beef
1 can (10¾ oz.) condensed
　tomato soup
1 can (8 oz.) tomato sauce
1 can (4 oz.) mushroom stems
　and pieces, drained
1 pkg. (1.5 oz.) dry spaghetti
　sauce seasoning mix
1 teaspoon salt
1 pkg. (8 oz.) lasagna noodles,
　cooked
1 carton (12 oz.) creamed cottage
　cheese
1 pkg. (6 oz.) sliced Mozzarella
　cheese
½ cup grated Parmesan cheese

1 Crumble sausage and ground beef into 1½-quart glass casserole. Cover with glass lid.

2 Microwave about **6 to 8 minutes** on **HIGH,** or until meat is browned; drain. Stir in soup, tomato sauce, mushrooms, seasoning mix and salt. Mix well. Layer in 12 x 7-inch glass baking dish: ⅓ cooked noodles, ⅓ meat mixture, ½ cottage cheese and ½ Mozzarella cheese. Repeat layers. On third layer of noodles, spread last ⅓ meat mixture and sprinkle with Parmesan cheese. Cover with wax paper.

3 Microwave **25 to 40 minutes** on **MED. HIGH (Roast),** or until hot in center (about 150°F.). Let stand, covered, 5 to 10 minutes. Cut in squares and serve.
6 to 8 Servings

Meats

CHOW MEIN

1 lb. coarsely ground beef and
    pork chow mein meat
2 small onions, chopped
3 stalks celery, chopped
½ medium green pepper,
    chopped
1 can (4 oz.) mushroom stems
    and pieces, undrained
1 can (16 oz.) bean sprouts,
    drained
2 tablespoons cornstarch
¼ cup soy sauce
1 tablespoon dark molasses
Chow mein noodles

1 Place meat in 3-quart glass casserole. Cover with glass lid.

2 Microwave for **10 minutes** on **HIGH.** Stir in onion, celery and green pepper. Drain liquid from mushrooms into small bowl; set aside. Stir mushrooms and bean sprouts into meat mixture. Combine remaining ingredients, except noodles, with drained mushroom liquid in small bowl until smooth; pour over meat; recover.

3 Microwave for **15 to 20 minutes** on **MEDIUM (Simmer),** or until meat is fork tender. Let stand, covered, 5 minutes before serving. Serve over chow mein noodles.
6 to 8 Servings

HOME-STYLE BEEF HASH

1 tablespoon butter or margarine
½ cup chopped onion
2 cups finely chopped or ground
    cooked beef
3 cups finely chopped cooked
    potatoes
1 package (¾ oz.) brown gravy
    mix
1 cup water
⅓ cup catsup
2 teaspoons Worcestershire
    sauce

1 Place butter and onion in 2-quart (8 x 8) glass baking dish.

2 Microwave for about **3 minutes** on **HIGH,** or until partly cooked. Stir in remaining ingredients. Cover with wax paper.

3 Microwave for **15 to 20 minutes** on **REHEAT,** or until hot (about 150° F.). Let stand, covered, 5 minutes before serving.
About 4 Servings

── MAKE-A-MEAL ──
Add Dessert—Hot Pink Pears

Prepare Reuben Casserole, recipe above through step 2. Place on rack in upper rack position.
Prepare Hot Pink Pears, recipe page 79, through step 1. Place pears on floor of oven not directly under the casserole.
Microwave **20 to 25 minutes** on **HIGH** or until casserole is hot. Baste the pears once during the cooking time. Let stand, covered, 5 minutes before serving. If softer pears are desired, continue cooking **3 to 5 minutes** on **HIGH** during the standing time for the casserole.

REUBEN CASSEROLE

1 can (16 oz.) sauerkraut, drained
1 can (12 oz.) corned beef, broken
    into small pieces
2 cups shredded Swiss cheese
½ cup mayonnaise or salad
    dressing
¼ cup bottled Thousand Island
    salad dressing
2 medium tomatoes, sliced
2 tablespoons butter or margarine
¼ cup pumpernickel bread
    crumbs

1 Place sauerkraut in 1½-quart glass casserole. Top with corned beef, then shredded cheese. Combine mayonnaise and Thousand Island dressing, spread over cheese. Top with tomato slices, set aside. Place butter in small glass bowl.

2 Microwave for about **1 minute** on **MED. HIGH (Roast),** or until melted. Stir in bread crumbs. Sprinkle buttered crumbs over tomato slices.

3 Microwave for **12 to 16 minutes** on **MED. HIGH (Roast),** or until heated through (about 150° F.). Let stand 5 minutes before serving.
About 6 Servings
TIP: Crumble about 2 slices dry pumpernickel bread to make crumbs.

VEAL PARMIGIANA

3 tablespoons butter or margarine
⅓ cup grated Parmesan cheese
3 tablespoons corn flake crumbs
½ teaspoon garlic salt
1 lb. veal cutlets or veal round
   steak, cut ½ inch thick
1 can (8 oz.) tomato sauce
½ teaspoon basil leaves
½ teaspoon oregano leaves
1 teaspoon Worcestershire sauce
2 slices Mozzarella cheese
Hot cooked spaghetti

1 Place butter in 2-quart (12 x 7) glass baking dish.

2 Microwave for about **1 minute** on **MED. HIGH (Roast),** or until melted. Combine Parmesan cheese, corn flake crumbs and garlic salt in flat dish. Cut veal into serving pieces. Dip each piece into butter; coat both sides with crumb mixture and set aside. Preheat microwave browning grill in oven on **HIGH** as directed for meats in manufacturer's instruction booklet. Lightly grease grill or spray it with vegetable coating. Place crumb-coated veal on hot grill.

3 Microwave for **2-3 minutes** on **HIGH.** Turn veal over and continue cooking for **2½ to 4 minutes** on **HIGH.** Meanwhile, combine remaining ingredients, except Mozzarella cheese and spaghetti, in greased glass baking dish. Add browned veal, turning to coat with tomato mixture. Cover with wax paper.

4 Microwave for **15 minutes** on **MEDIUM (Simmer).** Place cheese on veal and continue cooking for **3 to 4 minutes** on **MEDIUM (Simmer),** or until cheese melts. Serve on bed of cooked spaghetti.
4 to 6 Servings

CHICKEN A LA KING

1½ cups milk
¼ cup unsifted all-purpose flour
1 teaspoon salt
Dash pepper
Dash hot pepper sauce
¼ cup butter or margarine
2 cups diced cooked chicken
1 jar (2 oz.) diced pimento,
   drained
1 tablespoon dried parsley flakes

1 Combine milk, flour and seasonings in 4-cup glass measure; beat with rotary beater until smooth. Add butter.

2 Microwave for **3 minutes** on **HIGH.** Beat well and continue cooking for **2 to 5 minutes** on **HIGH,** or until thickened (about 180° F.). Stir in remaining ingredients.

3 Microwave for **2 to 4 minutes** on **REHEAT,** or until hot (about 150° F.). Stir and let stand 3 minutes before serving.
About 3 Cups Chicken à la King

MAKE-A-MEAL
Add a Vegetable

Prepare Chicken A LA KING through step 1. Place sauce on rack in lower rack position.
Place 1 can (16 oz.) favorite canned vegetable in small casserole; cover. Place vegetable on floor of oven. Microwave **3 minutes** on **HIGH.** Beat sauce well and continue cooking for **3 to 5 minutes** on **HIGH,** or until sauce is thickened. Stir remaining chicken ingredients into sauce and continue cooking **3 to 5 minutes** on **HIGH** or until hot.

SHRIMP CREOLE

2 tablespoons butter or margarine
5 green onions, sliced
½ cup chopped green pepper
1 clove garlic, finely chopped
1 can (16 oz.) whole tomatoes
1 can (6 oz.) tomato paste
1 teaspoon salt
1 teaspoon sugar
2 teaspoons dried parsley flakes
2 teaspoons Worcestershire
   sauce
¼ teaspoon paprika
⅛ teaspoon hot pepper sauce
1 package (10 oz.) frozen cooked
   shrimp
Hot cooked rice

1 Place butter, onions, green pepper and garlic in 2-quart glass casserole.

2 Microwave for about **3 minutes** on **HIGH,** or until vegetables are partly cooked. Stir in remaining ingredients, except cooked rice. Cover with glass lid.

3 Microwave for **5 minutes** on **REHEAT.** Stir, recover and continue cooking for **7 to 11 minutes** on **REHEAT,** or until hot (about 150° F.). Let stand, covered, 5 minutes before serving. Serve over hot cooked rice.
About 4 Servings

Meats

Remember the basics when microwaving meats—shielding, turning, arrangement, standing time, etc. for superior results.

Meat	Cut/Amount	Utensil	First Time and Setting	Second Time and Setting	Special Techniques
Bacon	(see page 48)				
Chops	Lamb Chops 1½ to 2 lb. (about 6 rib chops)	Microwave browning grill	**HIGH 8 min.**	**HIGH 7 to 11 min.**	Cut 1-inch thick; preheat grill. Turn over after first cooking time.
	Pork Chops 1 lb.	Microwave browning grill	**HIGH 6 min.**	**HIGH 5 to 11 min.**	Cut ½-inch thick; preheat grill. Turn over after first cooking time.
Ham & Picnics	Bone-in Ham, fully-cooked 7 to 8 lb.	13 x 9-inch glass baking dish with microwave roasting rack	**MED. HIGH (Roast) 8 to 11 min. per lb.** (about 120°F.)*	—	Turn over once.
	Boneless Ham, fully-cooked 2 to 5 lb.	12 x 7-inch glass baking dish with microwave roasting rack	**MED. HIGH (Roast) 11 to 13 min. per lb.** (about 120°F.)*	—	4 to 5 lb., turn over once.
	6 to 8 lb.	13 x 9-inch glass baking dish with microwave roasting rack	**MED. HIGH (Roast) 10 to 12 min. per lb.** (about 120°F.)*	—	Turn over once.
	Canned Ham 3 lb.	12 x 7-inch glass baking dish with microwave roasting rack	**MED. HIGH (Roast) 10 to 13 min. per lb.** (about 120°F.)*	—	—
	5 lb.		**MED. HIGH (Roast) 11 to 13 min. per lb.** (about 120°F.)*	—	—
	Cured Picnic (pork shoulder), fully cooked 3 to 5 lb.				Follow technique for boneless ham, fully cooked, above.
	Fresh Ham 3 to 5 lb.	4-quart glass ceramic Dutch oven	**HIGH 5 min. per lb.**	**MEDIUM (Simmer) 15 to 16 min. per lb.** (Well done, about 170°F.)*	Add ¼ cup water; cover tightly with glass lid.
	Fresh Picnic (pork shoulder) 2 to 2½ lb.	10-inch glass ceramic casserole	**HIGH 5 min. per lb.**	**MEDIUM (Simmer) 15 min. per lb.**	Add ¼ cup water; cover tightly with glass lid. Turn over once.
	Southern-type Ham, fully cooked 6 to 8 lb.				Prepare ham according to package instructions and follow technique for boneless ham, fully cooked, above.
Hamburger Patties (see pages 26 and 27)					
Hot Dogs (see page 55)					

Meat	Cut/Amount	Utensil	First Setting and Time	Second Setting and Time	Special Techniques
Ribs	Pork Spareribs & Country Style Ribs 2 to 3 lb.	13 x 9-inch glass baking dish	**MED. HIGH (Roast) 15 to 17 min. per lb.**	—	Brush with barbecue sauce during final cooking time, if desired.
Roasts, Less Tender (see pages 62 and 63)					
Roasts, Tender	Beef Rolled Rib 3 to 6 lb. or Beef Standing Rib 5 to 6 lb.	12 x 7-inch glass baking dish with microwave roasting rack	**HIGH 5 min. per lb.** **HIGH 6 min. per lb.** **HIGH 7 min. per lb.**	**MED. HIGH (Roast) 3 to 6 min. per lb.** (Rare, about 125°F.)* **MED. HIGH (Roast) 4 to 7 min. per lb.** (Medium, about 145°F.)* **MED. HIGH (Roast) 5 to 8 min. per lb.** (Well done, about 155°F.)*	Turn over once.
	Lamb Leg or Shoulder Roast 4 to 4½ lb.	12 x 7-inch glass baking dish with microwave roasting rack	**MED. HIGH (Roast) 14 to 16 min. per lb.** (Well done, about 180°F.)*	—	For rolled roasts, increase cooking time **1 min. per lb.**
	Pork Loin Roast, boneless 4 to 5 lb.	12 x 7-inch glass baking dish with microwave roasting rack	**HIGH 6 min. per lb.**	**MED. HIGH (Roast) 5 to 8 min. per lb.** (Well done, about 160°F.)*	Turn over once.
	Pork Loin, center rib 4 to 5 lb.	13 x 9-inch glass baking dish with microwave roasting rack	**HIGH 5 min. per lb.**	**MED. HIGH (Roast) 4 to 7 min. per lb.** (Well done, about 160°F.)*	Turn over once.
	Veal Rump 2 to 5 lb.	12 x 7-inch glass baking dish with microwave roasting rack	**MED. HIGH (Roast) 18 to 20 min. per lb.** (Well done, about 160°F.)*	—	Over 4 lb., turn over once.
Sausage (see pages 49 and 50)					
Steaks	Beef Flank Steak 1½ lb.	Soaked clay pot with lid	**HIGH 5 min. per lb.**	**MEDIUM (Simmer) 12 min. per lb.**	Turn over after first cooking time. Cover.
	Beef Rib-Eye Sirloin or T-Bone Steak 1½ to 2 lb.	Microwave browning grill	**HIGH 5 min.**	**HIGH 1 to 2 min.** or to desired doneness	Preheat grill; turn over after first cooking time.
	Beef Round Steak 1½ to 3 lb.	Soaked clay pot with lid	**HIGH 5 min. per lb.**	**MEDIUM (Simmer) 30 min. per lb.**	Turn over after first cooking time. Cover.

*Temperatures before standing time

Meats

You'll enjoy these delicious meat recipes. So easy now with your microwave oven.

BARBECUED SPARERIBS

2½ to 3 lb. pork spareribs
   cut into serving pieces
1 medium onion, chopped
½ medium green pepper,
chopped
2 cloves garlic, finely chopped
¼ cup catsup
½ cup packed brown sugar
¼ cup dark molasses
¼ cup lemon juice
1 teaspoon dry mustard

1 Place ribs in 13 x 9-inch glass baking dish. Cover with wax paper.

2 Microwave **15 minutes** on **MED. HIGH (Roast).** Drain and turn ribs over. Sprinkle with onion, green pepper and garlic. Combine remaining ingredients, pour over ribs. Recover and continue cooking **25 to 30 minutes** on **MED. HIGH (Roast),** or until fork tender Let stand, covered, 5 minutes before serving.
4 to 6 servings

ORIENTAL BEEF

1½ to 2 lb. beef sirloin steak,
   cut into thin strips
½ lb. fresh mushrooms, sliced
1 cup chopped onion
1 cup bias-cut celery
1 can (8 oz.) water chestnuts,
   drained and sliced
2 tablespoons cornstarch
¼ cup soy sauce
1 pkg. (6 oz.) frozen pea pods

1 Place all ingredients, except cornstarch, soy sauce and pea pods, in 3-quart glass casserole. Combine cornstarch and soy sauce in small bowl until smooth; stir into meat mixture. Cover with glass lid or wax paper.

2 Microwave **15 minutes** on **MED. HIGH (Roast).** Stir; add pea pods. Recover and continue cooking **5 to 10 minutes** on **MED. HIGH (Roast),** or until meat is fork tender. Stir to combine pea pods. Let stand, covered, 5 minutes before serving. **About 4 Servings**

CORNED BEEF AND CABBAGE

2¾ to 3 lb. corned beef brisket
   with seasonings
1 medium onion, sliced
1 small head cabbage, cut
   into wedges

1 Place corned beef brisket in water-soaked clay pot. Sprinkle with seasonings included with meat; add onion. Cover with water-soaked lid.

2 Microwave **30 minutes** on **MEDIUM (Simmer).** Turn brisket over; add cabbage and recover. Continue cooking **60 to 65 minutes** on **MEDIUM (Simmer),** or until meat is fork tender. Let stand, covered, 5 minutes before serving.
4 to 6 Servings

Pictured: Corned Beef and Cabbage, recipe above.

BRAISED RUMP ROAST

3½ to 4 lb. boneless beef rump
   roast
¼ cup dry red wine or water
1 large onion, sliced
2 teaspoons instant beef bouillon
1 teaspoon salt
⅛ teaspoon pepper

1 Place roast, fat-side-down, in water-soaked clay pot. Add wine and sprinkle on remaining ingredients; cover with water-soaked lid.

2 Microwave for **15 minutes** on **HIGH.** Turn roast over; recover.

3 Microwave for **55 to 65 minutes** on **MEDIUM (Simmer),** or until meat is fork tender. Let stand, covered, 10 minutes before serving.
9 to 12 Servings

PEPPER STEAK

1½ lbs. top round steak, cut into
   thin strips
1 teaspoon salt
⅛ teaspoon pepper
¼ cup soy sauce
2 green peppers, sliced
1 tablespoon cornstarch
¼ cup water
Tomato wedges, if desired

1 Place meat in 2-quart glass casserole. Sprinkle with salt and pepper; add soy sauce. Stir in green pepper. Cover with glass lid or wax paper.

2 Microwave for **14 to 16 minutes** on **HIGH.** Combine cornstarch and water in small bowl until smooth; stir into meat mixture. Recover and continue cooking for **2 to 4 minutes** on **HIGH,** or until thickened. Let stand, covered, 5 minutes before serving. Garnish with fresh tomato wedges.
About 4 Servings

MAKE-A-MEAL
Add Rice

Prepare Pepper Steak through step 1. Place meat mixture on rack in lower rack position.
Slit top of pouch (10 oz.) frozen rice. Place rice on floor of oven not directly under the meat mixture.
Microwave for **16 minutes** on **HIGH.** Stir cornstarch and water into meat mixture; recover. Microwave **4 to 8 minutes** on **HIGH** or until sauce has thickened. Let stand 5 minutes before serving. Continue cooking the rice for about 3 minutes during the standing time for the Pepper Steak if needed.

BEEF STROGANOFF

1 to 1½ lbs. beef sirloin steak, cut
   into cubes
1 medium onion, sliced and
   separated into rings
1 clove garlic, finely chopped
1 can (10½ oz.) condensed beef
   broth
1 can (4 oz.) whole mushrooms,
   drained
1 tablespoon snipped chives
2 tablespoons cornstarch
¼ cup dry red wine or water
1 carton (8 oz.) sour cream
Hot buttered noodles

1 Place meat, onion and garlic in 10-inch glass ceramic skillet. Cover with glass lid or wax paper.

2 Microwave for **8 to 10 minutes** on **HIGH.** Stir in broth, mushrooms and chives. Combine cornstarch and wine in small bowl until smooth; stir into broth. Recover.

3 Microwave for **18 to 22 minutes** on **MED. HIGH (Roast),** or until meat is fork tender. Mix in sour cream; recover, and continue cooking for 3 to 4 minutes on **MED. HIGH (Roast),** or until heated through. Let stand, covered, 5 minutes. Serve with hot buttered noodles.
About 4 Servings

RECIPE VARIATIONS

DILL STROGANOFF: Substitute 1 teaspoon dill weed for chives.

BEEF BURGUNDY: Omit chives and sour cream. Substitute ½ cup beef broth for can of condensed beef broth. Increase dry red wine to ¾ cup. Add 1 medium green pepper, cut into strips, 1 can (16 oz.) whole onions, drained, 1 teaspoon salt and ⅛ teaspoon pepper with mushrooms in basic recipe.

Meats

ITALIAN BEEF SHORT RIBS

3 lbs. beef short ribs
1 jar (15½ oz.) spaghetti sauce
1 small onion, chopped
1 teaspoon oregano leaves

1 Place ribs in water-soaked clay pot. Add sauce, onion and oregano. Cover with water-soaked lid.

2 Microwave for **15 minutes** on **HIGH.** Rearrange ribs; recover.

3 Microwave for **55 to 60 minutes** on **MEDIUM (Simmer),** or until meat is fork tender. Let stand, covered, 5 minutes before serving.
4 to 6 Servings

GLAZED COUNTRY-STYLE PORK RIBS

3 lbs. Country-Style pork spareribs
1 cup packed brown sugar
¼ cup vinegar
3 tablespoons Dijon mustard

1 Arrange ribs in 3-quart (13 x 9) glass baking dish. Cover with wax paper.

2 Microwave for **15 to 20 minutes** on **MED. HIGH (Roast).** Drain off fat. Combine remaining ingredients in small bowl; mix well, and pour over ribs. Recover and continue cooking for **35 to 40 minutes** on **MED. HIGH (Roast),** or until fork tender. Let stand, covered, 5 minutes before serving.
4 to 6 Servings

BARBECUED INDIVIDUAL MEAT LOAVES

2 lbs. ground beef
1 cup quick-cooking rolled oats
¾ cup bottled barbecue sauce
1 egg
2 tablespoons bottled Italian salad dressing
1½ teaspoons salt
¼ teaspoon pepper

1 Combine all ingredients in medium mixing bowl. Form into 8 individual meat loaves. Place in 2-quart (12 x 7) glass baking dish.

2 Microwave for **25 to 30 minutes** on **MED. HIGH (Roast),** or until meat is well done (about 140° F.). Let stand 5 minutes before serving.
6 to 8 Servings

MAKE-A-MEAL
Add Boiled Potatoes

Prepare Barbecued Individual Meat Loaves through step 1. Place meat loaves on rack in lower rack position.
Peel and quarter 4 potatoes. Place in an 8 x 8 inch baking dish with ½ cup water; cover with plastic wrap. Place on floor of oven.
Microwave for **25 to 30 minutes** on **HIGH** or until meat loaves are done (about 140° F.). Let meat loaves stand 5 minutes before serving. Continue cooking potatoes during the stand time for the meat loaves.

CHEESY BEEF-STUFFED PEPPERS

3 large green peppers, cut in half lengthwise
1 lb. ground beef
1 cup creamed cottage cheese
1 can (8 oz.) tomato sauce
1 small onion, finely chopped
1 egg
⅓ cup bread crumbs
1 tablespoon Worcestershire sauce
2 teaspoons salt
1 cup shredded process American cheese

1 Place peppers in 2-quart (12 x 7) glass baking dish; set aside. Combine remaining ingredients, except shredded cheese, in medium mixing bowl; mix well. Spoon meat mixture into green pepper halves. Cover with wax paper.

2 Microwave for **25 to 30 minutes** on **MED. HIGH (Roast),** or until meat is well done (about 140° F.). Top with shredded cheese and continue cooking on **MED. HIGH (Roast)** until cheese is melted.
About 6 Servings

RECIPE VARIATION

CABBAGE ROLLS: Substitute 8 large cabbage leaves for green peppers. Wash and stack leaves on glass plate; soften for **3 to 5 minutes** on **HIGH.** Substitute ¼ cup wheat germ for bread crumbs; omit shredded American cheese. Divide meat mixture among cabbage leaves; roll up, and place in 2-quart (12 x 7) glass baking dish. Serve topped with your favorite tomato sauce.

SPICY FLANK STEAK

1 tablespoon butter or margarine
1 tablespoon snipped chives
1 tablespoon prepared
    horseradish
½ teaspoon salt
½ teaspoon dry mustard
¼ teaspoon garlic powder
1½ to 2 lb. beef flank steak

1 Place butter in small glass bowl.

2 Microwave for about **1 minute** on **MED. HIGH (Roast)** or until melted. Stir in remaining ingredients except flank steak. Brush both sides of steak with butter mixture; place in water-soaked clay pot. Cover with water-soaked lid.

3 Microwave for **10 minutes** on **HIGH.** Turn steak over; recover.

4 Microwave for **20 to 30 minutes** on **MEDIUM (Simmer)** or until meat is fork tender. Let stand, covered, 5 minutes before serving.
About 4 Servings

RECIPE VARIATION:

BLEU CHEESE FLANK STEAK:
Substitute ¼ cup crumbled bleu cheese for horseradish and 1 teaspoon Worcestershire sauce for dry mustard. Place butter and cheese in small glass mixing bowl. Microwave as directed.

PORK ROAST WITH CHERRY SAUCE

4 to 5-lb. pork loin center rib roast
Cherry Sauce
½ cup cherry preserves
¼ cup dark corn syrup
2 tablespoons vinegar
⅛ teaspoon salt
⅛ teaspoon nutmeg
⅛ teaspoon cinnamon
⅛ teaspoon ground cloves
Dash pepper

1 Place roast, fat-side-down on microwave roasting rack, in 2-quart (12 x 7) glass baking dish.

2 Microwave for **25 minutes** on **HIGH.** Turn fat-side-up.

3 Microwave for **30 to 50 minutes** on **MED. HIGH (Roast),** or until meat registers 165° F. Let stand, covered with foil, 10 minutes before serving. Slash pork roast between ribs; place on serving platter. Pour hot Cherry Sauce over meat.

Cherry Sauce: Combine all sauce ingredients in 2-cup glass measure. Microwave for **3 to 5 minutes** on **MED. HIGH (Roast),** or until bubbly (about 150° F.).
6 to 8 Servings

STUFFED PORK CHOPS

4 pork chops (about 2½ lbs.), cut
    1 inch thick
½ cup orange marmalade
Orange Stuffing
1 tablespoon butter or margarine
2 tablespoons orange juice
2 green onions, sliced
1 cup dry seasoned bread stuffing
    cubes
1 teaspoon dried parsley flakes
1 teaspoon grated orange rind
Dash pepper
½ medium orange, chopped

1 Slit into side of each chop to form an opening or pocket. Divide Orange Stuffing among chops; stuff opening. Place chops in 10-inch glass ceramic skillet or shallow glass baking dish. Brush with orange marmalade. Cover with wax paper.

2 Microwave for **25 to 30 minutes** on **MED. HIGH (Roast),** or until fork tender. Let stand, covered, 5 minutes before serving.

Orange Stuffing: Place butter in medium glass mixing bowl. Microwave for about **1 minute** on **MED. HIGH (Roast),** or until melted. Add remaining ingredients; toss to combine.
4 Servings

Meats

CANADIAN BACON

1½ lbs. whole Canadian-style
   bacon, fully cooked
Whole cloves
½ cup applesauce
½ teaspoon cinnamon

1 Score fat on one side of bacon. Place bacon, scored-side-up, in (9 x 5) glass loaf dish. Insert cloves in top of bacon. Combine remaining ingredients and spread over top.

2 Microwave for **10 minutes** on **MED. HIGH (Roast).** Combine remaining ingredients and spread over top.

3 Microwave for **10 to 20 minutes** on **MED. HIGH (Roast),** or until meat is heated through (about 120° F.). Let stand 5 minutes.
About 7 Servings

BRATWURST IN BEER

4 uncooked bratwurst (about 1 lb.)
½ cup finely chopped onion
1 can (12 oz.) beer, room
   temperature

1 Place bratwurst in 9-inch round glass baking dish. Add remaining ingredients; cover with wax paper.

2 Microwave for **15 to 18 minutes** on **MED. HIGH (Roast),** or until meat is done (about 170° F.). Let stand, covered, 5 minutes before serving.
About 4 Servings

PINEAPPLE-GLAZED HAM LOAF

1 lb. ground ham
½ lb. ground pork
1½ cups dry bread crumbs
¾ cup milk
2 eggs, beaten
½ teaspoon dry mustard
2 teaspoons dried parsley flakes
Pineapple Glaze
1 can (8 oz.) crushed pineapple,
   undrained
¼ cup brown sugar

1 Combine all ham loaf ingredients in medium mixing bowl; mix well. Pat into (9 x 5) glass loaf dish.

2 Microwave for **30 to 35 minutes** on **MED. HIGH (Roast).** Pour Pineapple Glaze over ham loaf and continue cooking for **5 to 10 minutes** on **MED. HIGH (Roast),** or until meat is done (about 160° F.). Let stand 5 minutes before serving.

Pineapple Glaze: Combine all ingredients in small mixing bowl; mix well.
5 to 6 Servings

GLAZED HAM SLICE

1½ lb. ham slice, fully cooked,
   about 1-inch thick
Orange Glaze
¼ cup orange juice
2 tablespoons honey
1 teaspoon grated orange rind
½ teaspoon ginger

1 Place ham slice in 2-quart (12 x 7) glass baking dish. Pour Orange Glaze over ham. Cover with wax paper.

2 Microwave for **12 to 14 minutes** on **MED. HIGH (Roast),** or until heated through (about 120° F.).

Orange Glaze: Combine all ingredients in 1-cup measure; mix well.
4 to 6 Servings

RECIPE VARIATION

DILL GLAZED HAM: Substitute 2 tablespoons mayonnaise or salad dressing, 2 tablespoons prepared mustard, 2 green onions, sliced, and ½ teaspoon dill weed for Orange Glaze ingredients.

Leg of Lamb and Baked Potatoes

Prepare Leg of Lamb through Step 1. Wash and pierce 6 potatoes; place on floor of oven with 3 on each side of the clay pot. Microwave for **15 minutes** on HIGH. Turn roast over; recover.
Microwave for **50 minutes** on MEDIUM. Baste roast; recover.
Microwave for **10 minutes** on MEDIUM, or until meat is fork tender. Remove roast and let stand, covered, 5 to 10 minutes before serving. Continue cooking the potatoes for 3 to 5 minutes on HIGH during the standing time of the roast, if necessary.

LEG OF LAMB WITH MINT
3½ to 4 lb. leg of lamb
1 medium onion, sliced
2 cloves garlic, finely chopped
1 teaspoon salt
1 tablespoon dried mint leaves
¼ teaspoon pepper
¼ cup mint sauce

1 Place lamb roast in water-soaked clay pot. Add onion and garlic; sprinkle with seasonings. Cover with water-soaked lid.

2 Microwave for **15 minutes** on **HIGH.** Turn roast over; recover.

3 Microwave for **50 minutes** on **MEDIUM (Simmer).** Turn roast; baste with mint sauce. Recover and continue cooking for **10 to 25 minutes** on **MEDIUM (Simmer)** or until meat is fork tender. Baste with mint sauce occasionally during last 15 minutes of cooking. Let stand, covered, 5 minutes before serving.
4 to 6 Servings

HERB LAMB STEAKS
2 tablespoons butter or margarine
2 teaspoons dried parsley flakes
1 teaspoon marjoram leaves
½ teaspoon salt
½ teaspoon rosemary leaves
2 tablespoons water
4 lamb shoulder steaks (1½ to 2 lbs.)

1 Place butter in small glass bowl; add remaining ingredients, except water and steaks.

2 Microwave for about **1 minute** on **HIGH,** or until butter is melted. Stir to combine.

3 Place lamb steaks in 10-inch glass ceramic skillet or shallow baking dish. Brush with herb-butter mixture. Add water; cover with glass lid.

4 Microwave for **10 minutes** on **HIGH.**

5 Microwave for **30 to 35 minutes** on **MEDIUM (Simmer),** or until fork tender. Let stand, covered, 5 minutes before serving.
About 4 Servings

VEAL SCALLOPINI
1½ lbs. veal round steak, cut into strips
¼ cup butter or margarine
1 can (4 oz.) mushroom stems and pieces, drained
1 small onion, thinly sliced and separated into rings
1 clove garlic, finely chopped
½ teaspoon salt
1 tablespoon cornstarch
½ teaspoon oregano leaves
¼ cup dry sherry or water
2 small tomatoes, cut into wedges

1 Place veal strips, butter, mushrooms, onion, garlic and salt in 10-inch glass ceramic skillet.

2 Microwave for **10 to 12 minutes** on **MED. HIGH (Roast).** Combine remaining ingredients, except tomatoes, in small bowl until smooth; stir into veal mixture. Add tomatoes. Cover with glass lid or wax paper.

3 Microwave for **15 to 20 minutes** on **MEDIUM (Simmer),** or until meat is fork tender. Let stand, covered, 5 minutes before serving.
4 to 5 Servings

Meats

VEAL MEATBALLS IN SPICY SAUCE

2 tablespoons butter or margarine
2 lbs. ground veal
¼ cup dry bread crumbs
1 clove garlic, finely chopped
2 teaspoons prepared mustard
⅛ teaspoon white pepper

Spicy Sauce:
1 can (6 oz.) tomato paste
⅔ cup water
½ cup wine vinegar
¼ cup lemon juice
2 tablespoons Worcestershire sauce
½ cup packed brown sugar
1 teaspoon dry mustard
1 teaspoon salt
¼ teaspoon chili powder

1 Place butter in 1-quart (12 x 7) glass baking dish.

2 Microwave for about **1 minute** on **MEDIUM HIGH (ROAST),** or until melted. Combine remaining meatball ingredients in medium mixing bowl. Shape into 18 (1-inch) balls and place in melted butter. Cover with wax paper.

3 Microwave for **8 minutes** on **MEDIUM HIGH (ROAST).** Drain, pour Spicy Sauce over meatballs. Recover and continue cooking **8 to 12 minutes** on **MEDIUM HIGH (ROAST),** or until meat is well done in center. Let stand, covered 5 minutes before serving.

Spicy Sauce: Combine sauce ingredients in 4-cup glass measure, mix well.
4 to 6 Servings

DILLED LAMB PATTIES

4 ground lamb patties (about 1½ lbs.)
1 carton (8 oz.) plain yogurt
½ teaspoon salt
½ teaspoon dill weed
¼ teaspoon garlic powder
Dash pepper
1 medium tomato, chopped
1 medium onion, chopped

1 Place lamb patties in 2-quart (8 x 8) glass baking dish. Cover with wax paper.

2 Microwave for **15 minutes** on **MED. HIGH (Roast).** Drain. Combine remaining ingredients in small bowl and pour over patties. Recover and continue cooking for **4 to 5 minutes** on **MED. HIGH (Roast),** or until meat is done. Let stand, covered, 5 minutes before serving.
4 Servings

LIVER, BACON AND ONIONS

4 slices bacon
2 medium onions, sliced
1 lb. baby beef liver, sliced
Salt
Pepper

1 Arrange bacon in single layer in 2-quart (12 x 7) glass baking dish.

2 Microwave for **4 to 6 minutes** on **HIGH,** or until crisp. Remove bacon; set aside. Coat liver slices with bacon drippings; arrange in baking dish. Add onions. Cover with wax paper.

3 Microwave for **14 to 18 minutes** on **MEDIUM (Simmer),** or until meat loses pink color. Crumble bacon over top. Let stand, covered, 5 minutes before serving.
About 4 Servings

CURRIED KIDNEYS

1 lb. beef kidneys, trimmed and diced
1 medium onion, chopped
1 can (10½ oz.) condensed beef consommé
2 tablespoons cornstarch
2 teaspoons curry powder
⅛ teaspoon pepper
Hot cooked rice

1 Wash kidneys and place in water-soaked clay pot. Combine remaining ingredients except rice and pour over kidneys. Cover with water-soaked lid.

2 Microwave for **5 minutes** on **HIGH.** Stir and recover.

3 Microwave for **10 to 17 minutes** on **MEDIUM (Simmer)** or until kidneys are cooked. Serve over hot cooked rice.
About 4 Servings

MAKE-A-MEAL
Add Fresh Broccoli

Prepare Liver, Bacon and Onions through step 2. Place on rack in lower rack position.
Wash and trim Broccoli. Place Broccoli in 12 x 7 baking dish with ¼ cup water. Place Broccoli on floor of oven.
Microwave for **15 to 20 minutes** on **HIGH** or until meat loses pink color. Let stand 5 minutes before serving. Continue cooking broccoli during standing time for liver if needed.

Pasta & Rice

Rice and pastas are the old-fashioned convenience foods that store easily—cook with little effort. Microwave rice or pasta by bringing water, salt and fat to a full, rolling boil on **HIGH,** then stir in the rice or pasta and microwave on **MEDIUM (Simmer)** to gently rehydrate these dried foods to a light, tender texture. Note that hot tap water comes to a boil fastest—and a small amount of fat added to the water prevents bubble-overs. Wild rice cooks most tender when presoaked two hours before cooking. Remember precooked rice and pasta reheats very well in a microwave oven (see page 36.). **TO COOK NOODLES** see page 70.

RICE PILAF

3 tablespoons butter or margarine
⅓ cup chopped onion
⅓ cup chopped green pepper
⅓ cup shredded carrot
1 cup water
1½ teaspoons instant chicken bouillon
¼ teaspoon salt
¼ teaspoon poultry seasoning
Dash pepper
1 cup quick-cooking rice

1 Combine all ingredients, except rice, in 2-quart glass casserole. Cover with glass lid.

2 Microwave for **5 to 8 minutes,** on **HIGH,** until boiling. Stir in rice; recover. Rest, covered, 5 minutes or until all water is absorbed. Stir and serve.
4 to 6 Servings

QUICK-COOKING RICE

1 cup water
1 tablespoon butter
¼ teaspoon salt
1 cup quick-cooking rice

1 Combine water, butter and salt in a 1-quart casserole. Cover with glass lid.

2 Microwave **3 to 5 minutes** on **HIGH,** until boiling. Stir in rice. Let stand covered 5 minutes or until all water is absorbed.

LONG GRAIN RICE

2 cups water
1 tablespoon butter
¼ teaspoon salt
1 cup long grain white rice

1 Combine water, butter and salt in 2-quart casserole. Cover with glass lid.

2 Microwave **4 to 8 minutes** on **HIGH** until boiling. Stir in rice; recover.

3 Microwave **15 to 17 minutes** on **MEDIUM (Simmer)** or until rice is tender. Let stand, covered, 5 minutes before serving.

SPAGHETTI

4 cups water
1 tablespoon cooking oil
1 teaspoon salt
1 pkg. (7 oz.) spaghetti

1 Combine water, oil, and salt in 3-quart casserole. Cover with glass lid.

2 Microwave **10 to 15 minutes** on **HIGH,** until boiling. Stir in pasta; recover.

3 Microwave **8 to 10 minutes** on **MEDIUM (Simmer)** or until spaghetti is tender. Drain, rinse with hot water and serve.

SPICY SPAGHETTI

1 lb. ground beef
1 package (12 oz.) bulk pork sausage
½ cup chopped onion
1 clove garlic, finely chopped
1 can (32 oz.) tomato juice
2 cans (6 oz. each) tomato paste
1 tablespoon sugar
1 tablespoon dried parsley flakes
1 teaspoon salt
½ teaspoon ground oregano
¼ teaspoon pepper
Cooked spaghetti
Grated Parmesan cheese

1 Crumble ground beef and sausage into 3-quart glass casserole. Stir in onion and garlic; cover with glass lid.

2 Microwave for **10 to 12 minutes** on **HIGH** or until meat is cooked; drain. Stir in remaining ingredients, except spaghetti and cheese; recover.

3 Microwave for **30 to 35 minutes** on **MEDIUM (Simmer)** or until hot (about 160°F.). Serve on hot spaghetti; top with Parmesan cheese.
About 8 Servings.

Pies

Light-colored, tender pastry shells and cookie or cracker crumb crusts microwave in a jiffy on **MED. HIGH (Roast).** Pastry shells and crumb crusts must be baked before a filling is added for microwave cooking or refrigeration. And all cooking must be done in glass pie plates. Do not cover pies during baking. Fillings, microwaved separately, are cooked in glass mixing bowls or glass measures. Heat 1 piece of refrigerator-temperature pie for **35 to 40 seconds** on **REHEAT.**

BAKED PASTRY SHELL
½ pkg. (11 oz.) pie crust mix or favorite pie crust recipe

1 Prepare pie crust mix or pie crust recipe as directed on package or in recipe. Line 9-inch glass pie plate. Flute edge; prick bottom and sides of crust with fork.

2 Microwave **6 to 6½ minutes** on **MED. HIGH (Roast),** or until brown spots just begin to appear in crust. Cool.

9-inch Pastry Shell
TIP: To enhance crust color, mix 1 or 2 drops of yellow food coloring into water before adding it to dry ingredients.

CHOCOLATE, VANILLA, GINGER OR GRAHAM CRUMB CRUSTS
¼ cup butter or margarine
2 tablespoons sugar
1¼ cups crushed chocolate wafers (about 20 wafers);
or 1¼ cups crushed vanilla wafers (about 30);
or 1¼ cups crushed gingersnaps (about 30);
or 1¼ cups graham crackers (about 11 rectangles)

1 Place butter in 9-inch round glass pie plate.

2 Microwave about **1 minute** on **MED. HIGH (Roast),** or until melted. Stir in remaining ingredients; mix well. Press into bottom and up sides of 9-inch pie plate.

3 Microwave **1 to 2½ minutes** on **MED. HIGH (Roast),** or until set. Cool before filling.

9-inch Crumb Crust
TIP: 9-inch glass pie plate may vary in volume; add another ¼ cup crumbs, if necessary.

ORANGE CHIFFON PIE
4 egg yolks
1 cup orange juice
1 envelope unflavored gelatin
½ cup sugar
¼ teaspoon salt
2 teaspoons grated orange rind
4 egg whites
¼ cup sugar
1 (9-inch) Baked Pastry Shell (above)
Whipped cream

1 Beat egg yolks in medium glass mixing bowl. Stir in orange juice, gelatin, sugar and salt.

2 Microwave **4 to 7 minutes** on **MED. HIGH (Roast),** or until gelatin dissolves (about 160° F.). Stir in grated orange rind. Cool until consistency of unbeaten egg whites. Beat egg whites in small mixer bowl until frothy. Gradually beat in ¼ cup sugar, beating until mixture forms stiff peaks. Fold egg whites into gelatin mixture. Pour into baked pastry shell. Refrigerate at least 4 hours. Garnish with whipped cream before serving.
9-inch Pie

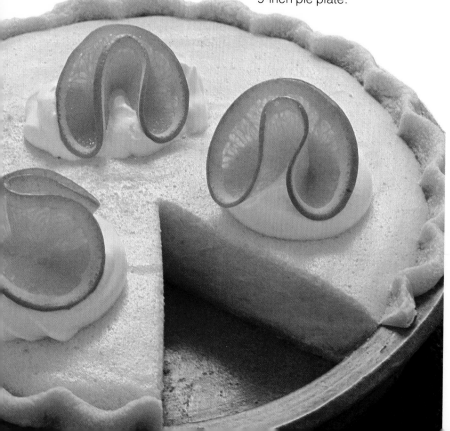

Pictured: Orange Chiffon Pie, recipe above.

RUBY RED STRAWBERRY PIE

¾ cup sugar
3 tablespoons cornstarch
½ cup water
1 package (10 oz.) frozen sliced
   strawberries, thawed
1 quart fresh strawberries,
   washed and hulled
1 (9-inch) Baked Pastry Shell,
   page 100
Whipped cream, if desired

1 Combine sugar, cornstarch and water in large glass mixing bowl until smooth; stir in strawberries and juice.

2 Microwave for **2 minutes** on **HIGH.** Stir and continue cooking for **2 to 5 minutes** on **HIGH,** or until thickened (about 190° F.). Cool. Fold whole strawberries into glaze mixture. Pour into baked pastry shell. Chill. Serve with whipped cream.
9-Inch Pie

TIP: Tip whole berries, point-up, for an easy-cutting attractive pie.

RECIPE VARIATION
GLAZED BLUEBERRY PEACH PIE: Substitute 3 cups peeled and sliced fresh peaches and 1 cup fresh blueberries for 1 quart fresh strawberries. Substitute 1 package (10 oz.) frozen sliced peaches, thawed, for strawberries.

BANANA CREAM PIE

1½ cups milk
⅔ cup sugar
3 tablespoons cornstarch
¼ teaspoon salt
4 egg yolks, slightly beaten
1 tablespoon butter or margarine
1 teaspoon vanilla
2 bananas, sliced
1 tablespoon lemon juice
1 (9-inch) Baked Pastry Shell in
   glass pie plate, page 100
Banana slices, if desired

1 Combine milk, sugar, cornstarch and salt in medium mixing bowl; beat with rotary beater until smooth.

2 Microwave for **4 minutes** on **HIGH.** Beat well and continue cooking for about **1 to 2 minutes** on **HIGH,** or until thickened (about 180° F.); beat well. Beat eggs and a small amount of hot milk in small bowl; beat into milk and sugar.

3 Microwave for **1½ to 2 minutes** on **MED. HIGH (Roast),** or until thickened (about 190° F.). Stir in butter and vanilla. Place banana slices in bottom of baked pastry shell; sprinkle with lemon juice. Pour cream mixture over bananas. Chill in refrigerator until set. Garnish with additional banana slices.
9-Inch Pie

RECIPE VARIATIONS
VANILLA CREAM PIE: Omit bananas and lemon juice. Garnish with orange slices.

COCONUT CREAM PIE: Substitute 1 cup shredded coconut for bananas and fold into cream mixture with butter and vanilla. Omit lemon juice. Top with toasted coconut.
CHOCOLATE CREAM PIE: Substitute 1 package (6 oz.) real chocolate pieces for bananas and stir into cream mixture with butter and vanilla until melted. Omit lemon juice. Top pie with whipped cream and chocolate shavings, if desired.

PECAN PIE

3 tablespoons butter or margarine
3 eggs, slightly beaten
1 cup dark corn syrup
¼ cup packed brown sugar
1½ teaspoons all-purpose flour
1 teaspoon vanilla
1½ cups pecan halves
1 (9-inch) Baked Pastry Shell in
   glass pie plate, page 100

1 Place butter in medium glass mixing bowl.

2 Microwave for about **1 minute** on **MED. HIGH (Roast),** or until melted. Stir in remaining ingredients, except Baked Pastry Shell; mix well; pour filling into shell.

3 Microwave for **20 to 25 minutes** on **MEDIUM (Simmer),** or until almost set in center. Let cool and set before serving.
9-Inch Pie

Poultry

For help in microwaving poultry, refer to the How-to on turkey on page 64. Also remember that poultry should be completely thawed before cooking. Wash bird, set aside giblets, then season cavity with salt and pepper before cooking, if desired. The metal clip holding drumsticks may be left in place on large birds during cooking. Pop-out "doneness indicators" do not indicate doneness but may be left in during microwave cooking. Place large whole poultry in glass or glass ceramic baking dish; poultry pieces in glass baking dishes or skillets. Use a microwave roasting rack when cooking whole birds.

Arrange pieces of poultry with thick edges toward the outside of the dish and as much as possible keep center of dish open. Arrange pieces of poultry skin-side-up; whole poultry breast-side-up. But if the recipe calls for turning, start cooking it breast-side-down. While whole poultry is cooked uncovered, pieces should be covered during cooking and standing time (unless a crumb coating is used or a crisper surface is desired). Use a glass lid or wax paper.

Foil may be used to cover portions of the meat, such as wings or drumsticks, that appear to be drying and darkening during cooking. (Do not allow foil to touch oven walls.) Doneness in all microwaved poultry is determined when meat cut near bone is no longer pink (about 180°F.). Check bone areas at both breast and thighs.

Remember, too, that cooking time may increase up to 15 minutes for birds above 8 pounds. (But 14 pounds is the maximum size for a bird in the microwave.) Standing time completes cooking of poultry. Allow whole birds or pieces totaling 10 pounds or less to stand 5 to 10 minutes after being taken from oven. Poultry over 10 pounds should stand 10 to 15 minutes. Cover tightly with foil during standing time. Cover cut-up poultry with a glass lid or wax paper.

Poultry	Weight	First Setting and Time	Special Techniques	Second Setting and Time
CHICKEN				
Whole, fryer	2 to 3 lb.	**HIGH** **7 to 8 min. per lb.** (about 180°F.)*	—	—
Whole, roasting	3 to 4 lb.	**HIGH** **8 to 9 min. per lb.** (about 180°F.)*	—	—
Quartered	2 to 3 lb.	**HIGH** **7 min. per lb.** (about 180°F.)*	—	—
Parts	1 to 2 lb.	**HIGH** **7 min. per lb.** (about 180°F.)*	Turn over wings and drumsticks	—
TURKEY				
Whole	8 to 10 lb.	**HIGH** **6 min. per lb.**	Turn over	**MED. HIGH (Roast)** **4 to 6 min. per lb.** (about 180°F.)*
	10 to 14 lb.	**HIGH** **6 min. per lb.**	Turn over	**MED. HIGH (Roast)** **4 to 6 min. per lb.** (about 180°F.)*
Breast, bone-in	4 to 5 lb.	**HIGH** **7 min. per lb.**	Turn over	**MED. HIGH (Roast)** **7 to 8 min. per lb.** (about 180°F.)*
Parts	2 to 3 lb.	**MED. HIGH (Roast)** **15 min. per lb.** (about 180°F.)*	Turn over wings and drumsticks	—
ROCK CORNISH GAME HEN				
Whole	4 (1 lb. ea.)	**HIGH** **8 to 9 min. per lb.** (about 180°F.)*	Turn over	—

*Temperatures are before standing time.

ORIENTAL CHICKEN

2 tablespoons butter or margarine
1/3 cup chopped green pepper
3 cups cooked rice
1 can (16 oz.) chow mein vegetables, drained
1 can (8 oz.) water chestnuts, drained and sliced
1 teaspoon soy sauce
2½ to 3 lb. quartered frying chicken

Pineapple Sauce

1/4 cup unsweetened pineapple juice
1 tablespoon cornstarch
1/4 cup honey
1/4 cup dry sherry or additional pineapple juice
1 tablespoon soy sauce
1/4 teaspoon ginger

1 Place butter and green pepper in 12 x 7-inch glass baking dish.

2 Microwave about **3 minutes** on **HIGH,** or until green pepper is partly cooked. Stir in remaining chicken ingredients, except chicken; spread in bottom of dish. Place chicken, skin-side-down and thick edges toward outside, over rice. Brush with ½ of Pineapple Sauce; cover.

3 Microwave **15 minutes** on **HIGH.** Turn chicken pieces over; brush with remaining sauce and continue cooking **13 to 15 minutes** on **HIGH,** or until meat cut near bone is no longer pink (about 180°F.). Let stand, covered, 5 minutes before serving.

Pineapple Sauce: Combine pineapple juice and cornstarch in 4-cup glass measure until smooth. Stir in remaining sauce ingredients. Microwave **2 to 3 minutes** on **HIGH,** or until thickened (about 200°F.). Stir well.
4 to 6 Servings

CHICKEN CACCIATORE

2½ to 3 lb. quartered frying chicken
1 small onion, thinly sliced and separated into rings
½ medium green pepper, cut into strips
1 can (28 oz.) whole tomatoes

Mushroom Sauce

2 tablespoons cornstarch
1/4 cup water
1 teaspoon sugar
½ teaspoon salt
2 cups reserved chicken broth
1 can (4 oz.) mushroom stems and pieces, drained

1 Arrange chicken pieces, skin-side-up and thick edges toward outside, in 12 x 7-inch glass baking dish. Place onion, green pepper and tomatoes over chicken. Cover with wax paper.

2 Microwave **35 to 40 minutes** on **HIGH,** or until meat cut near bone is no longer pink (about 180°F.). Drain, reserving 2 cups broth; set aside. Let stand, covered, 5 minutes before serving.

Mushroom Sauce: Combine all sauce ingredients, except mushrooms and broth, in 4-cup glass measure; beat with rotary beater until smooth. Beat in reserved broth. Microwave **2 to 3 minutes** on **HIGH.** Beat; add mushrooms and continue cooking **2 to 5 minutes** on **MED. HIGH (Roast),** or until thickened (about 200°F.). Stir well and pour over chicken to serve.
4 to 6 Servings

CHICKEN WITH DRIED BEEF

3 whole chicken breasts (1 lb. each), halved
1 can (10¾ oz.) condensed cream of mushroom soup
½ cup sour cream
1 jar (2½ oz.) dried beef, cut into pieces
1 tablespoon dried parsley flakes

1 Place chicken breasts skin-side-down and thick edges toward outside in 12 x 7-inch glass baking dish. Cover with plastic wrap.

2 Microwave on **HIGH** for **10 minutes;** drain. Combine remaining ingredients in medium mixing bowl. Turn chicken over; pour on sauce; recover.

3 Microwave on **MED. HIGH (Roast)** for **15 to 18 minutes** or until chicken is fork tender. Let stand, covered, 5 minutes before serving.
About 6 Servings

MAKE-A-MEAL
Add Vegetable

Prepare Chicken with Dried Beef through step 1; place on rack in lowest rack position.
Place 1 can (12 to 17 oz.) favorite vegetable in small casserole; cover. Place on floor of oven.
Microwave **10 minutes;** drain chicken. Turn chicken over; pour sauce on chicken. Recover.
Microwave **15 to 20 minutes** on **HIGH** or until chicken is fork tender. Let stand 5 minutes before serving.

Poultry

Coatings give chicken flavor, variety and an attractive look. There are two basic types—sauce and crumb coatings—and they're both here for you to try. (For fewer calories, remove skin and fat from chicken before coating.)

SEASONED CRUMB CHICKEN

¼ cup butter or margarine
¾ cup crushed rich round
   crackers (about 16 crackers)
½ cup grated Parmesan cheese
1 tablespoon dried parsley flakes
½ teaspoon garlic powder
⅛ teaspoon pepper
2½ to 3 lb. quartered frying
   chicken

1 Place butter in 12 x 7-inch glass baking dish.

2 Microwave about **1 minute** on **MED. HIGH (Roast),** or until melted. Combine remaining ingredients, except chicken, in flat dish. Roll chicken in melted butter, then in seasoned crumbs. Place chicken pieces, skin-side-up and thick edges toward outside, in buttered baking dish. Sprinkle with remaining bread crumbs.

3 Microwave **20 to 25 minutes** on **HIGH,** or until meat cut near bone is no longer pink (about 180° F.). Let stand 5 minutes before serving.
4 to 6 Servings

BARBECUE CHICKEN

2½ to 3 lb. quartered frying
   chicken
Barbecue Sauce
½ cup bottled barbecue sauce
¼ cup bottled Italian salad
   dressing
2 teaspoons dried parsley flakes

1 Combine barbecue sauce ingredients in small mixing bowl or 1-cup glass measure. Mix well and set aside.

2 Brush both sides of chicken quarters with sauce and place skin-side-up and thick edges toward the outside, in 12 x 7-inch glass baking dish.

3 Microwave **18 to 23 minutes** on **HIGH,** or until meat cut near bone is no longer pink. Let stand 5 minutes before serving.
4 to 6 Servings

COATING MIX CHICKEN

3 tablespoons cooking oil
2½ to 3 lb. frying chicken, cut up
1 pkg. (2⅜ oz.) seasoned coating
   mix

1 Brush chicken with oil. Pour coating mix into shallow dish. Roll chicken pieces in seasoned coating. Place chicken pieces, skin-side-down and thick edges toward outside, in 12 x 7-inch glass baking dish.

2 Microwave on **HIGH** for **12 minutes.** Turn chicken over and continue cooking on **HIGH** for **10 to 12 minutes** or until fork tender. Let stand 5 minutes before serving.
4 to 6 Servings

Pictured: Seasoned Crumb Chicken, Barbecue Chicken, Coating Mix Chicken, recipes above.

MAKE-A-MEAL

Roasted Chicken, Rice and Fresh Green Beans

Prepare Savory Chicken through step 1. Place chicken on rack in lower rack position.
Place 2 cups cooked rice in small casserole; cover. Wash and remove ends of 2 cups of green beans; place in small casserole with ¼ cup water; cover. Place rice and beans on floor of oven.
Microwave **25 to 35 minutes** on **HIGH** or until meat cut near bone is no longer pink (about 180° F.). Let stand 5 minutes before serving. Continue to cook green beans during the standing time for the chicken and rice if needed.

SAVORY CHICKEN

2½ to 3-lb. whole frying chicken
Salt
Pepper
1 small onion, chopped
1 stalk celery, chopped

Basting Sauce
¼ cup butter or margarine
½ teaspoon celery salt
½ teaspoon thyme leaves
¼ teaspoon rubbed sage

1 Wash chicken; set aside giblets. Sprinkle body cavity with salt and pepper. Place onion and celery in cavity. Tie legs together and wings to body. Place chicken, breast-side-up on microwave roasting rack, in 2-quart (12 x 7) glass baking dish. Brush with Basting Sauce.

2 Microwave for **20 to 26 minutes** on **HIGH,** or until meat cut near bone is no longer pink (about 180° F.). Let stand, covered with foil, 5 minutes before serving.
Basting Sauce: Place butter in 2-cup glass measure. Microwave for about **1 minute** on **MED. HIGH (Roast),** or until melted. Stir in remaining sauce ingredients.
4 to 6 Servings

CREAMY CHEESY CHICKEN

2½ to 3-lb. quartered frying chicken
¼ lb. fresh mushrooms, sliced
1 small onion, chopped
1 cup chicken broth
¼ cup dry white wine

Cheese Sauce
½ cup light cream
½ cup unsifted all-purpose flour
½ teaspoon garlic salt
1½ cups reserved chicken broth
1 cup shredded Cheddar cheese
2 tablespoons chopped pimento
2 teaspoons dried parsley flakes

1 Place chicken, skin-side-up and thick edges toward outside, in 2-quart (12 x 7) glass baking dish. Sprinkle on mushrooms and onion; pour chicken broth and wine over chicken. Cover with wax paper.

2 Microwave for **22 to 30 minutes** on **MED. HIGH (Roast),** or until meat cut near bone is no longer pink (about 180° F.). Drain, reserving 1½ cups broth; set aside. Let stand, covered, 5 minutes. Pour Cheese Sauce over chicken to serve.
Cheese Sauce: Combine cream, flour and garlic salt in 4-cup glass measure; beat with rotary beater until smooth. Beat in reserved broth; stir in remaining sauce ingredients. Microwave for **3 minutes** on **MED. HIGH (Roast).** Beat and continue cooking for **2 to 3½ minutes** on **MED. HIGH (Roast),** or until thickened (about 170°F.). Beat lightly.
4 to 6 Servings

BACON-GARLIC CHICKEN BREASTS

¼ cup butter or margarine
1 clove garlic, finely chopped
2 teaspoons dried parsely flakes
1 teaspoon grated lemon rind
¼ teaspoon salt
⅛ teaspoon hot pepper sauce
2 whole chicken breasts (1 lb. each), halved
4 bacon slices, cut in half

1 Place butter and garlic in 2-quart (12 x 7) glass baking dish.

2 Microwave for about **1 minute** on **HIGH,** or until garlic is partly cooked. Add remaining ingredients, except chicken breasts and bacon; mix well. Roll chicken breasts in seasoned butter; arrange, skin-side-up and thick edges toward outside, in buttered baking dish. Lay 2 half slices of bacon on each chicken breast.

3 Microwave for **14 to 18 minutes** on **HIGH,** or until meat cut near bone is no longer pink (about 180° F.). Let stand 5 minutes before serving.
4 Servings

Poultry

COUNTRY CHICKEN 'N RICE

1 cup chopped celery
1 cup thinly sliced carrots
3 green onions, sliced
1 can (16 oz.) whole tomatoes
1 tablespoon dried parsley flakes
2 teaspoons salt
Dash pepper
2½ to 3-lb. stewing chicken, cut up
3 cups water
1¾ cups uncooked rice

1 Combine all ingredients, except rice, in 3-quart glass casserole. Cover with glass lid.

2 Microwave for **20 minutes** on **HIGH** (about 160° F.). Turn chicken pieces over; recover.

3 Microwave for about **50 to 60 minutes** on **MEDIUM (Simmer),** or until meat cut near bone is no longer pink. Remove chicken from broth; set aside. Stir in rice; recover, and continue cooking broth for **15 to 20 minutes** on **MEDIUM (Simmer),** or until rice is cooked. Remove chicken from bones. Return meat to broth; mix well, and recover.

4 Microwave for **2 to 3 minutes** on **REHEAT,** or until hot (160° F.). Let stand, covered, 5 minutes before serving.
4 to 6 Servings

BARBECUED TURKEY DRUMSTICKS

2 to 2½ lbs. frozen turkey drumsticks, thawed
½ cup chili sauce
¼ cup white vinegar
2 tablespoons cooking oil
¼ cup chopped onion
¼ cup chopped green pepper
2 tablespoons packed brown sugar
1 tablespoon prepared mustard
1 teaspoon salt
½ teaspoon chili powder
⅛ teaspoon pepper

1 Place turkey drumsticks, thick end toward outside, in 2-quart (12 x 7) glass baking dish. Combine remaining ingredients in small mixing bowl; mix well. Pour sauce over drumsticks. Cover with wax paper.

2 Microwave for **20 minutes** on **MED. HIGH (Roast).** Turn drumsticks over; recover, and continue cooking for **17 to 22 minutes** on **MED. HIGH (Roast),** or until meat cut near bone is no longer pink (about 180° F.). Let stand, covered, 5 minutes before serving.
3 to 4 Servings

┌─ MAKE-A-MEAL ─┐
Crunchy Apple Crisp
Prepare Country Chicken 'n Rice through step 2. Place chicken on rack in lower rack position. Prepare Crunchy Apple Crisp, recipe page 79, through step 2. Place apple crisp on floor of oven. Microwave **50 to 60 minutes** on **MEDIUM (Simmer)** or until meat cut near bone is no longer pink. Remove chicken from broth; stir in rice. Recover. Microwave **15 to 23 minutes** on **HIGH** or until rice is done. Remove chicken meat from bones and stir into broth. Reheat **2 to 3 minutes** if needed.

TURKEY BREAST MADEIRA

3½ to 4-lb. frozen bone-in turkey breast, thawed
Madeira Glaze
½ cup red currant jelly
2 tablespoons Madeira or apple juice

1 Place turkey breast, skin-side-up on microwave roasting rack, in 2-quart (12 x 7) glass baking dish. Brush with ½ of Madeira Glaze.

2 Microwave for **40 minutes** on **HIGH.** Brush with remaining glaze and continue cooking for **35 to 40 minutes** on **MED. HIGH (Roast),** or until meat cut near bone is no longer pink (about 180° F.). Some areas may cook more rapidly than others; cover these with small pieces of foil to slow cooking. Let stand, covered with foil, 10 minutes before serving.

Madeira Glaze: Combine all glaze ingredients in small mixing bowl; beat with rotary beater until smooth.
8 to 12 Servings

Basic Stuffing

Try these delightful stuffing recipes the next time you want to prepare a special, festive meal. We've also included some recipes to "dress up" chicken pieces, too.

BASIC BREAD STUFFING

⅔ cup butter or margarine
½ cup chopped onion
1½ cups chopped celery
10 cups day-old soft bread cubes
1 tablespoon dried parsley flakes
1 teaspoon salt
½ teaspoon rubbed sage
¼ teaspoon poultry seasoning
⅛ teaspoon pepper

1 Place butter, onion and celery in 3-quart glass casserole.

2 Microwave **4 to 6 minutes** on **HIGH,** or until vegetables are partly cooked. Stir in cooked rice mix; mix well. Stuff poultry.

Stuffs 8 to 9 lb. Bird (6 to 8 Servings)

TIP: Microwave a casserole stuffing by blending ¾ to 1 cup chicken broth into basic recipe ingredients. Place in buttered 2-quart glass baking dish or casserole. Cover with glass lid or wax paper. Microwave **12 to 17 minutes** on **MEDIUM (Simmer),** or until hot (about 160° F.). Let stand, covered, 5 minutes before serving.

RECIPE VARIATIONS
PRUNE-ALMOND STUFFING
Decrease onion to ¼ cup and celery to 1 cup. Add 1 cup chopped prunes and ½ cup slivered almonds to basic recipe.

APPLE-SAUSAGE STUFFING
Add 1 package (12 oz.) bulk pork sausage, cooked and crumbled, and 1 small apple, chopped.
Stuffs 14 lb. Bird

WILD RICE STUFFING

3 tablespoons butter or margarine
¼ cup chopped celery
¼ cup chopped onion
¼ cup chopped green pepper
1 pkg. (6 oz.) white and wild rice mix, cooked

1 Place all ingredients, except rice, in 2-quart glass casserole.

2 Microwave **3 to 5 minutes** on **HIGH,** or until vegetables are partly cooked. Stir in remaining ingredients; mix well. Stuff poultry.

Stuffs 4 to 5 lb. Bird

TIP: 3 cups cooked wild rice may be substituted for white and wild rice mix. Season to taste.

Pictured: Turkey, chart page 102;
Apple-Sausage Stuffing, recipe above.

Poultry

DUCKLING WITH PEACH SAUCE

4 to 5-lb. frozen young duckling, thawed
1 orange unpeeled and quartered
1 small onion, quartered
Peach Glaze and Sauce
1 can (16 oz.) sliced peaches
¼ cup water
¼ cup orange juice
½ cup packed brown sugar
1 tablespoon cornstarch
1½ teaspoons dry mustard
⅛ teaspoon ground cloves

1 Wash duckling; set aside giblets. Stuff duckling neck and body cavity with orange and onion quarters. Secure openings with toothpicks or metal skewers. Tie legs together and wings to body. Place duckling, breast-side-up on microwave roasting rack, in 2-quart (12 x 7) glass baking dish. Brush with Peach Glaze.

2 Microwave for **45 to 55 minutes** on **MED. HIGH (Roast),** or until meat cut near bone is no longer pink (about 180° F.). Let stand, covered with foil, 10 minutes. Serve Peach Sauce over duckling.

Peach Glaze and Sauce: Drain peaches, reserving ½ cup juice; set aside peaches. Combine ½ cup reserved juice and remaining glaze ingredients in 4-cup glass measure; beat with rotary beater until smooth. Microwave for **2 minutes** on **HIGH.** Beat and continue cooking for **30 seconds to 1½ minutes** on **HIGH,** or until thickened (about 200° F.). Divide in half; add peach slices to one half for Peach Sauce. Use other half for Peach Glaze.
4 to 6 Servings

TURKEY BAKE

1 cup mayonnaise or salad dressing
2 tablespoons dry white wine, if desired
1 tablespoon lemon juice
½ teaspoon onion salt
5 cups cubed cooked turkey
2 cups finely chopped celery
1 jar (2 oz.) diced pimento, drained
¼ cup slivered almonds
2 green onions, sliced
1 can (3 oz.) French-fried onion rings

1 Combine mayonnaise, wine, lemon juice and onion salt in 2-quart glass casserole until smooth. Stir in remaining ingredients, except onion rings; mix well.

2 Microwave for **5 minutes** on **MED. HIGH (Roast).** Stir well; top with onion rings, and continue cooking for **3 to 4 minutes** on **MED. HIGH (Roast),** or until hot (about 140° F.). Let stand 3 minutes before serving. **6 to 8 Servings**

RECIPE VARIATIONS

CHICKEN BAKE: Substitute 5 cups cubed cooked chicken and ¼ cup chopped cashews for turkey and almonds.
HAM BAKE: Omit wine and lemon juice. Substitute 2 teaspoons prepared horseradish for onion salt. Substitute 4 cups finely chopped cooked ham for turkey; add 1 cup shredded Swiss cheese. Increase cooking time in basic recipe by 4 minutes. Serve on pineapple rings; garnish with parsley sprig.
CRAB BAKE: Decrease mayonnaise to ¾ cup and wine to 1 tablespoon. Substitute 1 teaspoon dill weed for onion salt. Substitute 1 can (6½ oz.) crab meat, drained; and 1 can (6½ oz.) tuna, drained, rinsed and flaked, for turkey. Add ½ cup finely chopped cucumber.

PHEASANT IN CREAM SAUCE

1½ to 2-lb. frozen pheasant, thawed and cut in half
Salt
Cream Sauce
1 package (3 oz.) cream cheese
1 can (10¾ oz.) condensed cream of onion soup
¼ cup dry white wine or water
2 tablespoons milk
½ cup shredded carrot
1 tablespoon dried parsley flakes
1 teaspoon instant beef bouillon

1 Wash pheasant and place, skin-side-down and thick edges toward outside, in 2-quart (8 x 8) glass baking dish. Sprinkle both sides of pheasant with salt. Cover with wax paper.

2 Microwave for **15 minutes** on **MED. HIGH (Roast).** Drain, turn pheasant over, and pour on Cream Sauce. Recover and continue cooking for **15 to 25 minutes** on **MED. HIGH (Roast),** or until meat cut near bone is no longer pink (about 180° F.). Let stand, covered, 5 minutes before serving.
Cream Sauce: Place cream cheese in medium glass mixing bowl. Microwave for about **30 seconds** on **MED. HIGH (Roast),** or until softened. Stir in remaining sauce ingredients; mix well.
2 to 3 Servings

Preserving Shortcuts

Need a few cups of jelly, preserves, pickles or relish now? Microwave some. These preserving techniques are designed for small batches of food stored in a refrigerator or freezer for a few days or weeks. **Use only conventional canning methods for processing** all food sealed in jars for shelf storage and for blanching large batches of food to be frozen or processed. Do not preserve meats or poultry in a microwave oven.

HARVEY'S DILL PICKLES

24 pickling cucumbers (3 to 4 inches each)
1 sweet red pepper, sliced
2 heads of fresh dill plant
4 cloves garlic
2 teaspoons pickling spices
1/8 teaspoon alum
Brine
1 cup vinegar
2 cups water
1/4 cup pickling salt

1 Wash cucumbers; cut off flower end. Cover with ice water; let stand 2 hours.

2 Divide red pepper, dill, garlic, pickling spices and alum between two 1-quart jars. Pack cucumbers into jars.

3 Combine Brine ingredients in 4-cup glass measure.

4 Microwave **10 to 15 minutes** on **HIGH,** until boiling (about 200° F.). Fill jars with hot brine mixture. Cool; cover, and refrigerate for at least 24 hours before serving. Pickles will keep up to 3 months in refrigerator.
2 Quarts Pickles

RASPBERRY PRESERVES

4 cups fresh raspberries, cleaned and washed
2½ cups sugar
2 tablespoons lemon juice
¼ bottle (6 oz.) liquid pectin

1 Combine raspberries, sugar and lemon juice in 1½-quart glass casserole.

2 Microwave for **7 minutes** on **MED. HIGH (Roast).** Stir and continue cooking for **8 to 11 minutes** on **MED. HIGH (Roast),** or until bubbly. Stir in pectin.

3 Fill glass jars; cool, and cover. Preserves will keep up to 4 months in refrigerator.
About 2 Cups Preserves
TIP: Substitute 2 packages (10 oz. each) frozen raspberries with sugar for fresh raspberries. Reduce sugar by ¼ cup and increase cooking time 5 to 6 minutes.

RECIPE VARIATION
STRAWBERRY PRESERVES: Substitute 4 cups fresh strawberries for raspberries in basic recipe. Or substitute 2 packages (10 oz. each) frozen strawberries with sugar; reduce sugar by ¼ cup, and increase cooking time 5 to 8 minutes.

VEGETABLE BLANCHING TECHNIQUE

4 cups water
½ lb. fresh vegetable

1 Place water in 2-quart glass casserole.

2 Microwave about **12 to 15 minutes** on **HIGH,** until boiling (about 200° F.). Drop vegetables into boiling water.

3 Microwave for ½ of regular cooking time on **HIGH**—see Vegetable Chart pages 116-118.

4 Chill in ice water immediately. Follow conventional freezing procedures, using only boilable, freezer bags. Check with your USDA Extension Service canning, preserving and freezing guides or freezer equipment manufacturers' guides for proper storage times and the blanching of special foods.

Puddings

How many hours have you spent standing and stirring at the range? Those days are gone now, because your microwave oven cooks puddings and custards quickly without scorching! Plus, you'll measure and microwave all in one glass cup. Just remember to microwave on **MEDIUM (Simmer),** because the eggs in these recipes are sensitive ingredients.

OLD-FASHIONED BREAD PUDDING

2 cups milk
2 eggs, slightly beaten
½ cup sugar
1 teaspoon cinnamon
¼ teaspoon salt
3 cups soft bread cubes
½ cup raisins
1 tablespoon butter or margarine

1 Combine milk, eggs, sugar, cinnamon and salt in 1½-quart glass casserole; beat with rotary beater. Stir in bread cubes and raisins. Dot with butter.

2 Microwave **26 to 28 minutes** on **MEDIUM (Simmer),** or until amost set in center. Let stand 5 minutes before serving.
4 to 6 Servings

RICE PUDDING WITH RAISINS

2½ cups milk
3 eggs, slightly beaten
½ cup sugar
1 tablespoon cornstarch
1 teaspoon vanilla
¾ teaspoon salt
½ teaspoon nutmeg
1½ cups cooked rice
½ cup raisins

1 Combine all ingredients in large mixing bowl; stir well. Pour into eight 6 oz. custard cups, filling each ¾ full.

2 Microwave **24 to 28 minutes** on **MEDIUM (Simmer),** or until almost set in center. If necessary, remove individual cups as they finish cooking and continue microwaving others until almost set. Let stand 5 minutes before serving.
8 Servings

BAKED CUSTARD

1¾ cups milk
¼ cup sugar
3 eggs
¼ teaspoon salt
½ teaspoon vanilla
Nutmeg

1 Place milk in 4-cup glass measure. Microwave **3½ to 4½ minutes** on **HIGH,** or until hot but not boiling. Add remaining ingredients except nutmeg; beat well with rotary beater. Pour into four 6 oz. glass custard cups, filling each ¾ full. Sprinkle with nutmeg.

2 Microwave **5½ to 10 minutes** on **MEDIUM (Simmer),** or until almost set in center. If necessary, remove individual custards as they finish cooking and continue microwaving others until almost set. Let stand 5 minutes before serving.

4 Custards
TIP: Custards may cook at slightly different rates because amount of custard in each cup tends to vary.

CHOCOLATE MOUSSE

2 squares (1 oz. ea.) semi-sweet chocolate
⅓ cup sugar
1 envelope unflavored gelatin
⅛ teaspoon salt
3 eggs, separated
1 cup milk
1 teaspoon vanilla
⅓ cup sugar
1 cup whipping cream, whipped

1 Place chocolate in large glass mixing bowl.

2 Microwave **1 to 3 minutes** on **HIGH,** or until melted. Stir in ⅓ cup sugar, gelatin, salt, egg yolks and milk. Beat well with rotary beater.

3 Microwave **4 minutes** on **MEDIUM (Simmer).** Beat and continue cooking **1 to 4 minutes** on **MEDIUM (Simmer),** or until slightly thickened. Beat in vanilla; refrigerate until cool.

4 Beat egg whites in small mixing bowl until soft peaks form. Gradually beat in ⅓ cup sugar until stiff peaks form. Fold egg whites and whipped cream into chocolate mixture. Spoon mixture into individual dishes. Chill about 3 hours or until set.
6 to 8 Servings

Salads

Your salad days are really here. Wilted lettuce salad dressings can be served really hot from a microwave without drying or scorching because microwaves cook from all directions, not just the bottom. Fruit salad dressing can be mixed, cooked and chilled in a single dish.

WILTED LETTUCE SALAD

5 slices bacon
¼ cup vinegar
1 tablespoon sugar
2 tablespoons water
½ teaspoon salt
¼ teaspoon dry mustard
⅛ teaspoon pepper
1 head leaf lettuce, torn apart
2 green onions, finely sliced

1 Arrange bacon slices in single layer in 12 x 7-inch glass baking dish.

2 Microwave **4 to 7 minutes** on **HIGH,** or until bacon is crisp. Drain bacon, reserving 2 tablespoons bacon drippings; crumble, and set aside. Combine reserved bacon drippings and remaining ingredients, except lettuce and onion, in small glass mixing bowl; mix well.

3 Microwave **2 to 4 minutes** on **HIGH,** or until hot (about 200°F.). Place lettuce and onion in salad bowl. Pour on hot dressing. Toss lightly to coat lettuce leaves. Sprinkle bacon over top; serve.

6 to 8 Servings

TIP: Add 2 chopped hard-cooked eggs when salad is tossed.

RECIPE VARIATION

WILTED SPINACH SALAD: Substitute 1 tablespoon brown sugar for sugar. Substitute 1 lb. fresh spinach, washed and torn apart, for leaf lettuce.

CARDAMOM FRUIT DRESSING

Use on fresh or canned fruit salads.

1 egg, beaten
1 cup orange juice
⅓ cup honey
1 tablespoon cornstarch
¼ teaspoon ground cardamom
2 tablespoons butter or margarine
½ cup whipping cream, whipped

1 Beat egg in 4-cup glass measure with rotary beater. Stir in remaining ingredients, except butter and whipping cream; beat well. Add butter.

2 Microwave **3 minutes** on **MED. HIGH (Roast).** Beat and continue cooking **2½ to 5 minutes** on **MED. HIGH (Roast),** or until thickened (about 200°F.). Beat lightly. Chill. Fold in whipped cream. Serve over fruit salad.

About 2 Cups Dressing

Pictured: Cardamom Fruit Dressing, recipe above, over fruit salad.

Salads

CLASSIC DRESSING

1 cup milk
1 tablespoon cornstarch
2 teaspoons sugar
1 teaspoon dry mustard
1 teaspoon salt
¼ teaspoon paprika
⅛ teaspoon pepper
1 egg yolk, beaten
2 tablespoons vinegar
¼ cup cooking oil

1 Measure milk in 4-cup glass measure. Add cornstarch, sugar and seasonings; beat with rotary beater until smooth.

2 Microwave for **3 minutes** on **HIGH.** Beat and continue cooking for **1 to 2½ minutes** on **HIGH,** or until thickened (about 200° F.). Beat well. Add small amount of warm mixture to beaten egg yolk. Stir and combine with remaining hot cream mixture.

3 Microwave for **2 to 3 minutes** on **MED. HIGH (Roast),** or until slightly thickened (about 180° F.). Stir in vinegar and oil. Beat until smooth. Store in the refrigerator up to a week.
About 1⅓ Cups Dressing
RECIPE VARIATIONS
GARDEN DRESSING: Add ⅓ cup finely chopped cucumber or zucchini and 1 tablespoon snipped chives with vinegar and oil.
EGG DRESSING: Add 2 chopped hard-cooked eggs and 1 teaspoon dried parsley flakes with vinegar and oil.
CREAMY DRESSING: Add ¼ cup sour cream and 1 teaspoon dried parsley flakes with vinegar and oil.

HOT APPLE SLAW

⅓ cup vinegar
¼ cup water
2 tablespoons sugar
1 teaspoon celery seed
1 teaspoon salt
6 cups shredded cabbage
1 small apple, finely sliced
2 tablespoons butter or margarine

1 Combine vinegar, water, sugar, celery seed and salt in 2-quart glass casserole. Toss with cabbage and apple slices. Dot with butter. Cover with glass lid.

2 Microwave for **4 to 6 minutes** on **HIGH,** or until heated through. Let stand, covered, 3 minutes. Toss and serve. **3 to 4 Servings**
TIP: Serve with cooked ham slices and Swiss cheese.

HOT GERMAN POTATO SALAD

8 slices bacon
6 green onions, sliced
½ cup chopped green pepper
⅓ cup vinegar
1 teaspoon sugar
1 teaspoon salt
Dash pepper
1 egg, beaten
5 cups sliced cooked potatoes

1 Arrange bacon in a single layer in 3-quart (13 x 9) glass baking dish.

2 Microwave for **7 to 10 minutes** on **HIGH,** or until bacon is crisp. Crumble bacon; set aside. Reserve ¼ cup bacon drippings; pour into 2-quart glass casserole. Add onions and green pepper.

3 Microwave for about **2 minutes** on **HIGH,** or until vegetables are partly cooked. Stir in vinegar and seasonings. Add beaten egg; mix well.

4 Microwave for **1 minute** on **MED. HIGH (Roast).** Stir well and continue cooking for about **30 to 60 seconds** on **MED. HIGH (Roast),** or until slightly thickened. Stir in potatoes and crumbled bacon. Cover with glass lid.

5 Microwave for **8 to 10 minutes** on **MED. HIGH (Roast),** or until hot.
About 6 Servings

Sauces

As in puddings and custards, microwaves don't scorch sauces, so constant stirring is eliminated. Since no evaporation occurs in microwaving, you'll notice that less liquid or more thickening is needed than in conventional sauce recipes. Thickenings must be thoroughly blended into microwave sauces to keep them smooth—and they must be cooked thoroughly. You can mix, measure and cook all in one glass measuring cup, too. But choose a size at least twice as large as the sauce's volume to allow for bubbling.

GRAVY

⅓ cup meat or poultry drippings
⅓ cup unsifted all-purpose flour
1¾ cups warm broth or water
Salt
Pepper

1 Combine drippings and flour in 4-cup glass measure. Add broth and beat with rotary beater until smooth. Season to taste.

2 Microwave on **HIGH** for **2 to 3 minutes.** Beat well and continue cooking **1½ to 3 minutes** on **HIGH,** or until thickened (about 200°F.). Beat lightly and serve.
About 2 Cups Gravy
TIP: For additional color, add 1 to 2 teaspoons soy sauce.

BASIC WHITE SAUCE

1 cup milk
3 tablespoons all-purpose flour
¼ teaspoon salt
⅛ teaspoon pepper
3 tablespoons butter or margarine

1 Combine all ingredients, except butter, in 4-cup glass measure; beat with rotary beater until smooth. Add butter.

2 Microwave **3 minutes** on **HIGH.** Beat well and continue cooking **1 to 2 minutes** on **HIGH,** or until thickened (about 175°F.). Beat lightly and serve.
About 1 Cup Sauce

RECIPE VARIATIONS

THIN WHITE SAUCE: Use 2 tablespoons all-purpose flour and 2 tablespoons butter or margarine in basic recipe.
THICK WHITE SAUCE: Use ¼ cup all-purpose flour and ¼ cup butter or margarine in basic recipe.
CHEESE SAUCE: Add ½ cup shredded process American cheese and ¼ teaspoon Worcestershire sauce with butter in basic sauce. Microwave **4 minutes** on **MED. HIGH (Roast).** Beat well and continue cooking **2½ to 4 minutes** on **MED. HIGH (Roast),** or until thickened (about 175°F.).Beat lightly and serve.
About 1¼ Cups Sauce
BECHAMEL SAUCE: Add 1 green onion, chopped and dash nutmeg with butter in basic recipe.
About 1 Cup Sauce
EGG SAUCE: Stir in 2 hard-cooked eggs, finely chopped, when basic sauce has been cooked. Microwave for an additional **1 to 2 minutes** on **MED. HIGH (Roast),** or until hot.
About 1½ Cups Sauce

FUDGE SAUCE

1 pkg. (6 oz.) semi-sweet "real" chocolate pieces
1 square unsweetened chocolate
⅓ cup butter or margarine
2 cups powdered sugar
2 cans (5 oz. ea.) evaporated milk
1 teaspoon vanilla

1 Place all chocolate and butter in 4-cup glass measure.

2 Microwave about **1½ to 2 minutes** on **MED. HIGH (Roast),** or until melted. stir in remaining ingredients; beat with rotary beater until smooth.

3 Microwave **5 to 8 minutes** on **MED. HIGH (Roast),** or until bubbly (about 200°F.). Serve warm.
About 2 Cups Sauce

Sauces

ORANGE SAUCE
¼ cup sugar
1 tablespoon cornstarch
Juice of 1 orange plus enough
  water to make 1 cup liquid
1 to 2 teaspoons grated orange
  rind
2 to 4 tablespoons Grand Marnier
  or other orange-flavored
  liqueur, if desired

1 Combine all ingredients,
  except liqueur, in 4-cup
  glass measure; beat with
rotary beater until smooth.

2 Microwave for **2 minutes** on
  HIGH. Beat well and
  continue cooking for **½ to
1½ minutes** on **HIGH,** or until
thickened (about 175° F.). Stir in
Grand Marnier.
About 1½ Cups Sauce

RECIPE VARIATION
LEMON SAUCE: Substitute juice
of 1 lemon and 1 tablespoon
grated lemon rind for orange juice
and orange rind in basic sauce.
Omit Grand Marnier.

PARSLEY BUTTER
¼ cup butter or margarine
2 tablespoons snipped fresh
  parsley or 1 tablespoon dried
  parsley flakes.
½ teaspoon lemon juice

1 Place butter in 1-cup glass
  measure.

2 Microwave for about **1
  minute** on **MED. HIGH
  (Roast),** or until melted. Stir
in parsley and lemon juice.
**About ¼ Cup Parsley Butter
TIP:** Any time you want to melt
butter without seasonings,
microwave for about **1 minute** on
MED. HIGH (Roast), or until
melted.

RECIPE VARIATIONS
CHIVE BUTTER: Substitute 1
tablespoon chopped fresh or
frozen chives for parsley and
lemon juice in basic recipe.
DILL BUTTER: Substitute ½
teaspoon dill weed for parsley
and lemon juice in basic recipe.
CHEESY GARLIC BUTTER:
Substitute 2 tablespoons grated
Parmesan cheese and ¼
teaspoon garlic powder for
parsley and lemon juice in basic
recipe.
ONION BUTTER: Substitute 1
tablespoon dry onion soup mix for
parsley and lemon juice in basic
recipe.

BASIC BROWN SAUCE
1 cup water
3 tablespoons all-purpose flour
¼ teaspoon salt
⅛ teaspoon pepper
3 tablespoons butter or margarine
1 small onion, finely chopped
1 teaspoon instant beef bouillon

1 Combine water, flour and
  seasonings in 4-cup glass
  measure; beat with rotary
beater until smooth. Add
remaining ingredients.

2 Microwave on **HIGH** for **3
  minutes.** Beat well and
  continue cooking for **1 to 1½
minutes** on **HIGH,** or until
thickened, (about 200° F.). Beat
lightly and serve.
About 1½ Cups Sauce

RECIPE VARIATIONS
BORDELAISE SAUCE: Add ¼
cup red Bordeaux wine and ⅛
teaspoon thyme leaves after first
cooking time in basic sauce. Beat
well and continue cooking for **2 to
3 minutes** on **HIGH,** or until
thickened (about 200° F.). Beat
lightly and serve.
About 1¾ Cups Sauce
CHASSEUR SAUCE: Add 1 jar
(2½ oz.) sliced mushrooms,
drained, ¼ cup dry white wine
and 1 tablespoon catsup after first
cooking time in basic sauce. Beat
well and continue cooking for **3½
to 4½ minutes** on **MED. HIGH
(Roast),** or until thickened (about
200° F.). Beat lightly and serve.
About 2 Cups Sauce
MADEIRA SAUCE: Add ¼ cup
Madeira or dry sherry, 1
tablespoon catsup and 1
teaspoon dried parsley flakes
after first cooking time in basic
sauce. Beat well and continue
cooking for **2 to 3 minutes** on
HIGH, or until thickened (about
200° F.). Beat lightly and serve.
About 1¾ Cups Sauce

Soup & Sandwich

There are three basic soup techniques. First, microwave soups made with raw vegetables on **HIGH** to retain flavor and color. Second, microwave soups made with uncooked meat or chicken on **HIGH** for fast heating, then finish on **MEDIUM (Simmer)** to blend flavors into broth and tenderize meat. Also use this **HIGH/MEDIUM (Simmer)** technique to soften and tenderize dried peas, beans and lentils in soup. Third, microwave soups made of cooked meat and/or vegetables on **REHEAT** so food holds shape and texture. Most canned soups are heated on **REHEAT.**

Microwave sensitive ingredients such as clams, cream, cheese or mushrooms on **MED. HIGH (Roast)** setting or lower to prevent "popping" or curdling.

Bread, rolls and taco shells all make great microwave sandwiches. Toasted bread makes the firmest base for hot sandwiches. Heat bread and rolls just until warm, not hot, or bread toughens. Taco shells freshen nicely when warmed for **15 to 20 seconds** on REHEAT.

TURKEY BROTH

Turkey gizzard, heart, liver and
   neck
3 cups water
½ teaspoon salt
⅛ teaspoon pepper
1 bay leaf

1 Combine all ingredients in 2-quart glass casserole. Cover with glass lid.

2 Microwave for about **15 minutes** on **HIGH.** Stir well and recover.

3 Microwave for **18 to 20 minutes** on **MEDIUM (Simmer),** or until flavors are blended (about 200°F.). Remove meat and bay leaf from broth. Use broth for soup or gravy. Let stand, covered, 5 minutes.
About 3 Cups Broth

VICHYSSOISE

2 medium potatoes, peeled and
   sliced
1½ cups thinly sliced Spanish
   onions or leeks
3 cups chicken broth
¼ cup unsifted all-purpose flour
½ teaspoon salt
Dash white pepper
¼ cup cold water
1 cup light cream

1 Place potatoes, onions and chicken broth in 2-quart glass casserole. Cover with glass lid.

2 Microwave for **13 to 19 minutes** on **HIGH,** or until potatoes are tender. Purée in electric blender or press through colander; return to casserole. Combine flour, seasonings and water in small bowl until smooth; stir into potato mixture.

3 Microwave **8 to 9 minutes** on **HIGH,** or until thickened (about 190°F.). Cool slightly and stir in cream. Chill and serve in soup bowls or cups.
4 to 6 Servings

TACOS

1 lb. ground beef
1½ teaspoons chili powder
½ teaspoon salt
½ teaspoon garlic powder
⅛ teaspoon cayenne pepper
¼ cup water
Taco shells
Cheddar cheese, shredded
Lettuce, shredded
Onion, finely chopped
Tomato, chopped

1 Crumble ground beef into 1½-quart glass casserole. Cover with glass lid.

2 Microwave for **5 minutes** on **HIGH;** drain. Stir in seasonings and water and continue cooking for **3 to 4 minutes** on **HIGH,** or until meat is well done.

3 Fill each taco shell with about 2 heaping tablespoons of meat filling. Top with remaining ingredients.
TIP: Taco shells can be heated for **15 to 30 seconds** on **REHEAT** before filling.

Vegetables

Here's a handy chart for microwaving fresh and frozen vegetables. When adapting one of your own conventional recipes, reduce liquids and cook as specified in the chart. Also, remember to slit the center of all frozen vegetable pouches before microwaving. Place frozen pouch in a glass baking dish or directly on the oven's bottom shelf. Place other frozen and fresh vegetables, in a glass baking dish or casserole. Arrange spear vegetables with the stalk end toward the outside of cooking dish. Add ¼ cup water when cooking fresh vegetables, except baked potatoes, squash or ears of corn. Cover dish with glass lid or plastic wrap. Microwave all fresh and frozen vegetables on **HIGH.** Vegetables may still seem firm when oven time finishes cooking. Allow them to stand 2 to 5 minutes depending on amount and density.

Vegetable	Preparation for Fresh Vegetables	Amount	Time on HIGH
Artichokes Wash thoroughly. Cut 1 inch off top, straight across. Remove any loose leaves around bottom. Remove thorns on each outer leaf by clipping about ½ inch off tips. Dip cut edges in lemon juice to prevent darkening. After cooking, remove prickly core with spoon.		**Fresh,** 3½ inches in diameter 1 2 3 4 **Frozen,** hearts, 10 oz. pkg.	**4 to 7** **7 to 10** **9 to 12** **11 to 14** **5 to 7**
Asparagus: Spears, cut Wash thoroughly to remove dirt and sand. Snap off tough stalk discarding base. Leave spears whole, cut or break into 1 to 2-inch pieces.		**Fresh** ¾ lb. 1½ lb. **Frozen** 9 oz. pouch 10 oz. pkg.	**5 to 6** **9 to 10** **6 to 7** **8 to 9**
Beans: Green and Wax Wash green and wax beans thoroughly; remove ends. Leave whole. Cut lengthwise into strips, break or cut into 1 to 2-inch pieces. Add about ¼ cup more water for softer beans.		**Fresh** 1 lb. 2 lbs. **Frozen,** French style or cut 9 oz. pkg. 10 oz. pouch	**12 to 14** **16 to 18** **8 to 9** **7 to 8**
Beans: Lima Remove beans from shell; wash thoroughly.		**Fresh** 1 lb. 2 lbs. **Frozen** 10 oz. pkg. 10 oz. pouch	**10 to 12** **14 to 16** **6 to 7** **7 to 8**
Beets Scrub beet with brush to remove dirt. Leave 1 inch of top attached to beet. Peel and cut off stem after beets are cooked.		**Fresh, whole** 4 medium	**14 to 18**
Broccoli Wash carefully, removing large outer leaves and tough portion of stalk. Slit stems to speed cooking.		**Fresh,** 1½ lb. **Frozen** 10 oz. pkg. 10 oz. pouch	**10 to 14** **8 to 9** **8 to 9**
Brussels Sprouts Discard wilted outer leaves, wash thoroughly. Cut off stem.		**Fresh** ½ lb. 1 lb. **Frozen** 8 oz. pkg. 10 oz. pouch	**5 to 8** **7 to 9** **6 to 8** **6 to 8**
Cabbage Wash and remove any wilted outside leaves. Add a little vinegar or lemon juice to red cabbage to retain color.		**Fresh,** shredded ½ medium 1 medium	**5 to 7** **8 to 11**

Vegetable	Preparation for Fresh Vegetables	Amount	Time on HIGH
Carrots Scrape or peel with vegetable peeler to remove thin layer of outer skin. Cut off tops and tips. Leave whole, slice, dice or sliver. Fresh, young, tender carrots microwave best.		**Fresh,** sliced, diced, slivered 2 medium 4 medium 6 medium	4 to 6 7 to 10 9 to 12
		Frozen, diced or whole	8 to 10
Cauliflower Remove outer leaves and excess part of stem. Wash thoroughly. Leave whole or cut into flowerettes.		**Fresh,** broken into flowerettes 1 medium	7 to 9
		Fresh, whole 1 medium 1 large	8 to 10 12 to 15
		Frozen 10 oz. pkg.	8 to 9
Celery Separate stalks and wash thoroughly. Cut off base and any blemishes. Slice or cut into strips.		**Fresh,** 1-inch slices or strips 6 stalks	8 to 10
Corn, Kernel Remove husk and silk; trim ends. Wash thoroughly. Cut corn off cob using sharp knife.		**Fresh,** cut from cob 1½ cups 3 cups	6 to 7 7 to 8
		Frozen 10 oz. pkg. 10 oz. pouch	6 to 7 5 to 8
Eggplant Wash and peel tough skin areas. Cut off stem. Leave whole, slice or dice. IMPORTANT! Pierce or prick skin if cooked whole.		**Fresh,** sliced or diced 1 medium	5 to 7
		Fresh, whole 1 medium	6 to 8
Okra Wash thoroughly and cut off stems.		**Fresh,** whole ½ lb.	4 to 6
		Fresh, sliced ½ lb.	3 to 5
		Frozen 10 oz. pkg.	7 to 9
Onions Peel and quarter.		**Fresh,** quartered 8 small 2 large 4 large	6 to 8 6 to 8 8 to 12
		Frozen, in cream sauce 10 oz. pouch	6 to 8
Peas, Black-Eyed		**Frozen** 10 oz. pkg.	9 to 11

Vegetables

Vegetable	Preparation for Fresh Vegetables	Amount	Time on HIGH
Peas, Green Shell peas, removing peas from pods. Wash thoroughly.		**Fresh** 2 lb. 3 lb.	**8 to 9** **10 to 11**
		Frozen 10 oz. pkg. 10 oz. pouch	**6 to 7** **6 to 7**
		Frozen, pods, 6 oz. pkg.	**3 to 4**
Potatoes, Sweet or Yams Wash and scrub thoroughly. **IMPORTANT!** Pierce or prick skin before cooking. Potatoes will feel firm before standing time.		**Fresh** 1 medium 2 medium 4 medium 6 medium	**4 to 5** **6 to 9** **8 to 11** **10 to 13**
Potatoes, Baked Wash and scrub thoroughly. To Bake: **IMPORTANT!** Pierce or prick skins of whole unpeeled potatoes before cooking. Cook directly on oven's bottom shelf. Use only fresh potatoes and do not overcook as extreme dehydration may cause smoke or fire. Potatoes feel firm when taken from oven (see pages 68 and 69). **NOTE:** Overcooking may result with only 10% longer cooking times than recommended. Always start with the minimum cooking times and **DO NOT** overcook. (See pages 6 and 7.)		**Fresh,** baking 1 medium (about 5 oz. each) 2 medium 4 medium 6 medium 8 medium 1 small (about 3 oz. each) 2 small 4 small 6 small 8 small	**4 to 5** **7 to 8** **10 to 15** **16 to 21** **22 to 26** **3 to 5** **4 to 6** **5 to 7** **7 to 9** **10 to 12**
Potatoes, Boiled Cook, peeled or unpeeled quartered potatoes in covered glass baking dish. Potatoes will feel firm before standing time.		**Fresh,** boiling, quartered 2 medium 4 medium	**10 to 11** **18 to 20**
Spinach Wash leaves, removing any wilted leaves or tough stems.		**Fresh,** 1 lb.	**6 to 7**
		Frozen, leaf or chopped 10 oz. pkg. 10 oz. pouch	**8 to 10** **7 to 9**
Squash, Acorn or Butternut Leave whole until cooked; cut and remove seeds before serving. **IMPORTANT!** Remember to pierce or prick unpeeled squash before cooking.		**Fresh,** whole 1 medium 2 medium	**8 to 12** **12 to 16**
Squash, Hubbard Wash and cut into serving pieces. Peel either before or after cooking.		**Fresh,** 6 x 6-inch piece **Frozen,** 12 oz. pkg.	**8 to 10** **6 to 9**
Squash, Zucchini Wash and slice thinly. Do not peel.		**Fresh,** ¼-inch slices 2 medium or 3 cups	**7 to 8**
Turnip Greens Wash leaves, removing any wilted leaves or tough stems.		**Fresh** 1 lb.	**6 to 7**
		Frozen 10 oz. pkg.	**7 to 9**
Vegetables, Mixed		**Frozen** 10 oz. pkg. 10 oz. pouch	**6 to 7** **6 to 7**

Garnishes and toppings move a serving bowl of steaming-hot vegetables all the way from ordinary to spectacular. (Use almonds, crumb toppings, bacon bits, cheese or maybe bean sprouts.) Mixing vegetables dresses up a meal, too. You'll want to experiment on your own, but start with these ideas...

TANGY MUSTARD CAULIFLOWER

1 medium head cauliflower
¼ cup water
½ cup mayonnaise or salad dressing
1 teaspoon finely chopped onion
1 teaspoon prepared mustard
¼ teaspoon salt
½ cup shredded Cheddar cheese

1 Place cauliflower and water in 1½-quart glass casserole. Cover with glass lid.

2 Microwave **9 minutes** on **HIGH.** Drain. Combine mayonnaise, onion, mustard and salt in small mixing bowl. Spoon mustard sauce on top of cauliflower. Sprinkle with cheese.

3 Microwave **1½ to 3 minutes** on **MED. HIGH (Roast),** to heat topping and melt cheese. Let stand 2 minutes before serving.
6 to 8 Servings

ZUCCHINI COMBO

3 medium zucchini or summer squash
2 cups (8 oz.) sliced fresh mushrooms
¼ teaspoon garlic powder
½ teaspoon salt
¼ cup butter or margarine
2 medium tomatoes, cut into wedges
¼ cup Parmesan cheese

1 Slice zucchini and combine with mushrooms in 1½-quart glass casserole. Sprinkle with garlic powder and salt; dot with butter.

2 Microwave, covered, **5 to 8 minutes** on **HIGH,** or until zucchini is tender. Stir in tomatoes and cheese.

3 Microwave, covered **2 to 3 minutes,** or until hot.
4 to 5 Servings

PEAS MANDARIN

1 pkg. (10 oz.) frozen peas
1 can (16 oz.) small whole onions, drained
¼ cup butter or margarine
1 tablespoon cornstarch
1 tablespoon honey
½ teaspoon salt
¼ teaspoon leaf rosemary, if desired
Dash pepper
1 can (11 oz.) mandarin oranges, drained

1 Microwave peas in 1½-quart covered glass casserole **4 to 5 minutes** on **MED. HIGH (Roast),** or until thawed; drain.

2 Stir in remaining ingredients, except oranges.

3 Microwave, uncovered, **5 to 8 minutes** on **MED. HIGH (Roast),** or until peas are tender. Stir in oranges.

4 Microwave about **1 to 2 minutes** on **MED. HIGH (Roast),** or until hot.
5 to 6 Servings

Pictured: Cauliflower, chart page 117; with cheese sauce, recipe page 113.

Vegetables

BEANS VINAIGRETTE

1 package (9 oz.) frozen cut green
    beans
1 package (9 oz.) frozen cut wax
    beans

Vinaigrette

¼ cup cooking oil
¼ cup tarragon vinegar or white
    vinegar plus dash tarragon
¼ cup grated Parmesan cheese
2 teaspoons snipped chives
½ teaspoon sugar
½ teaspoon salt
¼ teaspoon pepper
Pimento strips, if desired

1 Place beans in medium glass
mixing bowl. Cover with wax
paper.

2 Microwave for **5 minutes** on
HIGH; stir. Microwave for **5
to 7 minutes** on **HIGH,** or
until tender-crisp; drain. Pour
Vinaigrette over beans, toss to
combine; cover. Chill about 8
hours, stirring occasionally.
Garnish with pimento strips.

3 **Vinaigrette:** Combine all
ingredients in 1-cup glass
measure.

4 to 6 Servings

BRUSSELS SPROUTS AU GRATIN

1 package (10 oz.) frozen brussels
    sprouts
1 small onion, thinly sliced
½ medium green pepper, cut into
    strips
1 can (4 oz.) mushroom stems
    and pieces, drained
½ teaspoon salt
4 slices process American
    cheese

1 Combine vegetables and salt
in 1½-quart glass casserole.
Cover with glass lid.

2 Microwave for **10 minutes**
on **MED. HIGH (Roast).**
Lay cheese slices over
vegetables; recover, and continue
cooking for about **3 to 4 minutes**
on **MED. HIGH (Roast),** or until
cheese melts. Stir in cheese. Let
stand, covered, 2 minutes before
serving.

About 4 Servings

RUSSIAN BEETS

5 medium uncooked beets, diced
3 tablespoons butter or margarine
2 tablespoons vinegar
½ teaspoon dill weed
½ teaspoon salt
¼ teaspoon pepper
3 tablespoons all-purpose flour
½ cup milk

1 Place all ingredients, except
flour and milk, in 1½-quart
glass casserole. Cover with
glass lid.

2 Microwave for **8 to 10
minutes** on **HIGH** or until
beets are almost tender.
Combine flour and milk in small
bowl until smooth; stir into beets,
and continue cooking for **4 to 6
minutes** on **HIGH,** or until
thickened. Let stand, covered, 2
minutes before serving.

4 to 6 Servings

TIP: Substitute 2 cans (16 oz.
each) beets, drained, for fresh
beets in basic recipe. Microwave
for **6 minutes** on **REHEAT.**
Combine flour and milk in small
bowl until smooth; stir into beets,
and continue cooking for **5 to 8
minutes** on **REHEAT,** or until
thickened. Let stand, covered, 2
minutes before serving.

BUTTER-CRUNCH BROCCOLI

1½ lbs. fresh broccoli
¼ cup water

Butter-Crunch Sauce:

1 cup water
1 tablespoon cornstarch
1 teaspoon instant chicken
    bouillon
2 teaspoons dried parsley flakes
¼ teaspoon salt
¼ cup butter or margarine
¼ cup chopped cashews

1 Arrange broccoli in 2-quart
(12 x 7) glass baking dish
with stalks toward outside of
dish. Add ¼ cup water. Cover
with wax paper; set aside.

2 Combine remaining
ingredients, except butter
and cashews, in 1½-quart
glass casserole; beat with rotary
beater until smooth. Add butter.

3 Place broccoli on upper
rack position of oven and
sauce on bottom shelf, in a
staggered arrangement.

4 Microwave both for **10
minutes** on **HIGH.** Beat
sauce and continue cooking
for **7 to 8 minutes** on **HIGH,** or
until broccoli is tender-crisp.
Remove broccoli and rack and
continue cooking sauce **2 to 4
minutes** on **HIGH,** until sauce has
thickened (about 175°F.). Stir
cashews into sauce. Let stand, 2
minutes: pour sauce over broccoli
to serve.

About 4 Servings

EASY POTATO BAKE

1 lb. frozen diced hash brown
   potatoes
1 can (10½ oz.) condensed cream
   of potato soup
½ cup sour cream
2 green onions, sliced
½ teaspoon salt
¼ teaspoon pepper
Paprika

1 Place frozen potatoes in
1½-quart glass casserole.
Cover with glass lid.

2 Microwave for **5 minutes** on
HIGH. Stir in remaining
ingredients, except paprika.
Sprinkle with paprika; recover.

3 Microwave for **12 to 14
minutes** on **MED. HIGH
(Roast),** or until hot (about
150° F.). Let stand, covered, 5
minutes before serving.
About 6 Servings

RECIPE VARIATIONS

PARTY POTATOES: Add 2
tablespoons chopped pimento
and 2 tablespoons chopped
green pepper to potato mixture in
basic recipe.
MUSHROOM POTATO: Add 1 jar
(2½ oz.) sliced mushrooms,
drained, and 2 teaspoons dried
parsley flakes to potato mixture in
basic recipe.

STUFFED BAKED POTATO

4 medium baking potatoes
2 tablespoons butter or margarine
½ cup milk
¼ teaspoon salt
Dash pepper
½ cup shredded process
   American cheese

1 Prick potatoes and place in
oven.

2 Microwave for **10 to 15
minutes** on **HIGH,** or until
tender. Cut potatoes in half.
Carefully scoop cooked potato
out of shells and place in medium
mixing bowl. Add butter, milk and
seasonings; mash until lump-free.
Fill potato shells; top with cheese
and place on glass serving
platter. Continue cooking for **4 to
7 minutes** on **MED. HIGH
(Roast),** or until hot (about
150° F.). Let stand 3 minutes
before serving.
4 to 8 Servings
TIP: Prepare stuffed potatoes
ahead of meal, arrange on
serving platter and refrigerate.
Microwave on **MED. HIGH
(Roast)** for **6 to 8 minutes** during
final cooking period in basic
recipe.

RECIPE VARIATIONS

ZIPPY BACON POTATOES: Stir ¼
cup process Cheddar-type
cheese spread with bacon and ½
teaspoon prepared horseradish
into mashed potato mixture. Fill
potato shells; omit shredded
cheese topping. Microwave for **6
to 8 minutes** on **MED. HIGH
(Roast),** during final cooking
period in basic recipe.
*BLEU CHEESE-ONION
POTATOES:* Stir ⅓ cup crumbled
Bleu cheese and 1 tablespoon
chopped green onion into
mashed potato mixture. Fill potato
shells, omit shredded cheese
topping. Microwave for **8 to 12
minutes** on **MED. HIGH (Roast)**
during final cooking period in
basic recipe.

MASHED POTATO PUFF

1½ cups water
2 tablespoons butter or margarine
½ cup milk
1½ cups instant potato flakes
1 cup creamed cottage cheese
1 cup shredded process
   American cheese
3 green onions, sliced
2 teaspoons prepared mustard
¼ teaspoon garlic salt
2 eggs, separated
¼ cup buttered dry bread crumbs

1 Place water and butter in
1½-quart glass casserole;
cover.

2 Microwave for about **2
minutes** on **HIGH,** or until
hot. Add milk; stir in
remaining ingredients, except
egg whites and crumbs. Beat
well.

3 Beat egg whites in small
mixing bowl until stiff peaks
form; fold into potato
mixture. Sprinkle with bread
crumbs.

4 Microwave for about **20
minutes** on **MED. HIGH
(Roast),** or until set (about
160° F.). Let stand 5 minutes
before serving.
4 to 6 Servings
**TIP: Buttered Bread
Crumbs**—Place 2 tablespoons
butter or margarine in 1-cup glass
measure. Microwave on **MED.
HIGH (Roast)** for about **1 minute.**
Stir in ¼ cup dry bread crumbs.

Vegetables

GERMAN RED CABBAGE

3 tablespoons lard or bacon
   drippings
6 cups shredded red cabbage
2 medium cooking apples, peeled
   and chopped
⅓ cup finely chopped onion
¼ cup packed brown sugar
⅓ cup wine vinegar
¼ cup water
1½ teaspoons salt
1 teaspoon caraway seed
¼ teaspoon pepper

1 Combine all ingredients in
2½-quart glass casserole.
Cover with glass lid.

2 Microwave for **8 minutes** on
HIGH. Stir well and continue
cooking for **8 to 9 minutes**
on **HIGH,** or until cabbage is
tender-crisp. Let stand, covered,
2 minutes before serving.
About 6 Servings

CREAMY DILLED CARROTS

2 packages (10 oz. each) carrot
   nuggets frozen in butter sauce
1 tablespoon all-purpose flour
⅓ cup milk
½ teaspoon dill weed

1 Place carrot pouches directly
on bottom shelf of oven or in
1½-quart glass casserole.
Slit pouches.

2 Microwave for **8 to 12
minutes** on **HIGH,** or until
carrots are hot. Empty carrot
pouches into 1½-quart glass
casserole. Combine remaining
ingredients in small bowl until
smooth; stir in carrots. Cover with
glass lid.

3 Microwave for **3 to 4
minutes** on **HIGH,** or until
sauce thickens (about
150°F.). Let stand, covered, 2
minutes before serving.
About 6 Servings

SWEET POTATO PECAN BALLS

3 medium sweet potatoes, peeled
   and quartered
¼ cup water
½ teaspoon salt
½ teaspoon nutmeg
1 egg, beaten
1¼ cups finely chopped pecans
¼ cup butter or margarine
½ cup packed brown sugar
3 tablespoons light corn syrup

1 Place sweet potatoes in
1½-quart glass casserole.
Add water; cover with glass
lid.

2 Microwave for **7 to 10
minutes** on **HIGH,** or until
tender. Drain; mash to give 2
cups. Stir in seasonings. Shape
mixture into 10 (2-inch) balls. Dip
each into beaten egg; roll in
chopped nuts, and arrange in
2-quart (12 x 7) glass baking dish.

3 Place butter in 2-cup glass
measure.

4 Microwave for about **1
minute** on **MED. HIGH
(Roast),** or until melted. Stir
in brown sugar and corn syrup.
Pour over potato balls.

5 Microwave for **4 to 8
minutes** on **HIGH,** or until
hot. Let stand 2 minutes
before serving.
About 4 Servings

ONION-FILLED SQUASH

2 medium acorn squash
1 package (10 oz.) frozen small
   onions in cream sauce
Salt
¼ cup bacon-flavored bits or 2
   slices bacon, crisply fried and
   crumbled
¼ cup chopped green pepper
¼ cup buttered bread crumbs

1 Pierce whole squash and set
aside.

2 Place slit pouch of frozen
onions in 1½-quart glass
casserole.

3 Place squash on upper rack
in oven and onions on
bottom shelf.

4 Microwave both for **6 to 8
minutes** on **HIGH,** or until
onions are warm. Remove
onions and continue cooking
squash for **4 minutes** on **HIGH.**

5 Cut squash in half; remove
seeds. Place, cut-side-up, in
2-quart (8 x 8) glass baking
dish; sprinkle with salt. Empty
onion pouch into casserole; stir in
bacon and green pepper. Fill
centers of squash with onion
mixture; sprinkle with bread
crumbs. Remove rack from oven.

6 Microwave squash for **10 to
11 minutes** on **HIGH,** or until
tender. Let stand 5 minutes
before serving.
4 Servings
**TIP: Buttered Bread
Crumbs**—Place 2 tablespoons
butter or margarine in 1-cup glass
measure. Microwave on **MED.
HIGH (Roast)** for about **1 minute.**
Stir in ¼ cup dry bread crumbs.

Adapting Recipes

Now that you have mastered the basics of microwave cooking and the advanced recipes...want to adapt an old family favorite to microwave cooking? Just follow these simple instructions:

1 Use the basic microwave information in your cookbook to determine whether your recipe is suitable to microwave cooking. (Some foods which require crisp, fried crust or dry surface should be done conventionally.)

2 If your recipe is suitable, find one in your cookbook with similar main ingredients. Note the technique and recommended time. If the quantities of the two recipes are similar, the times and the techniques will be much the same. If your recipe has larger or smaller quantities the time should be adjusted accordingly.

3 Begin with ¼ conventional cooking time. Add more if required.

4 To avoid boil-overs, use a larger dish than is specified in your conventional recipe.

5 Reduce the liquid in your recipe by ¼ since liquid does not evaporate during microwave cooking as it does in conventional cooking.

6 Use slightly less seasoning, especially with strong flavors. This can be corrected to taste later.

7 When adapting a recipe using rice or noodles, use quick-cooking rice or precooked noodles, or other ingredients combined with them may overcook before the rice or noodles are tender.

8 When adapting a family favorite that serves 8 to 10 people cut the recipe in half for adapting purposes. Later, use the successfully adapted recipe in original large quantity.

For more detailed information and examples of how to adapt conventional recipes to microwave cooking you may want to purchase the cookbook *Microwave Cooking: Adapting Conventional Recipes*. Others in this series include *Microwave Meats, Baking & Desserts, Microwave Cooking on a Diet, Everyday Dinners in a Half Hour,* and *Fruits & Vegetables.* See your local microwave dealer or bookstore for these and further titles in this continuing series.

Index

126